THE GLASS SEED

THE GLASS SEED

THE FRAGILE BEAUTY OF HEART, MIND & MEMORY

EILEEN DELEHANTY PEARKES

timeless books 2007

FOR

Mary Virginia Arnold Delehanty
November 28, 1931 – June 6, 2007

with love and gratitude

timeless books
www.timeless.org

In Canada:
Box 9, Kootenay Bay, BC V0B 1X0
contact@timeless.org
(800) 661-8711

In the United States:
P.O. Box 3543, Spokane, WA 99220-3543
info@timeless.org
(800) 251-9273

Cover photograph by Andrea Rollefson
Design by Todd Stewart www.breeree.com

Printed in Canada
Interior stock: 100% post consumer waste recycled acid-free paper
Cover stock: FSC certified 10% post consumer waste recycled paper

Library and Archives Canada Cataloguing in Publication

Pearkes, Eileen Delehanty, 1961-
    The glass seed : the fragile beauty of heart, mind and
memory / Eileen Delehanty Pearkes.

Includes bibliographical references.
ISBN 978-1-932018-18-9

    1. Pearkes, Eileen Delehanty, 1961-. 2. Mothers and
daughters. 3. Spiritual healing. 4. Spirituality. I. Title.

PS8631.E32Z465 2007   C818'.603   C2007-905217-7

TABLE OF CONTENTS

AND SO IT IS with our own past. It is a labour in vain to attempt to recapture it: all the efforts of our intellect must prove futile. The past is hidden somewhere outside the realm, beyond the reach of intellect, in some material object (in the sensation which that material object will give us) which we do not suspect. And as for that object, it depends on chance whether we come upon it or not before we ourselves must die.

– Marcel Proust, *Swann's Way*

ALZHEIMER'S DISEASE STAGES OF DECLINE

Functional Assessment Staging developed by Dr. Barry Reisberg

STAGE	LOST ABILITY
1	No difficulty at all
2	Subjective memory trouble does not affect job/home
3	Some difficulty maintaining job performance
4	Some difficulty to hold a job, prepare meals, handle personal finances
5	Some difficulty to select proper clothing for occasion or season
6A	Some difficulty to put on clothes properly
6B	Some difficulty to adjust bath water temperature
6C	Some difficulty to use toilet cleanly without assistance
6D	Some difficulty to maintain urinary continence
6E	Some difficulty to maintain fecal continence
7A	Speech limited to six or so words per day
7B	Speech limited to about one word per day or fewer
7C	Can no longer walk without assistance
7D	Can no longer sit up without assistance
7E	Can no longer smile
7F	Can no longer hold up head or the head is frozen with contractures

Reisberg, B. *Functional Assessment Staging (FAST)*. Psychopharmacology Bulletin, 1988; 24:653-659. © 1984 by Barry Reisberg, M.D. Reproduced with permission.

AUTUMN/WINTER 2001

MEMORY & HER MUSES

THE TAFFETA SKIRT GLISTENS like a current of water, falling in shimmering, chartreuse lengths to the floor. It is the colour of earliest spring, of being fully alive again. A velvet, persimmon-orange bodice attaches to the glistening green fabric. The bodice has been seeded with thousands of tiny glass beads of the same warm colour and looks as if it should fit tightly, to display the weight and shape of a woman's breasts. I reach out to touch the bead-crusted surface. The sparkling beauty of the dress fills me with a strange desire.

A woman in attendance behind the shop counter sees that I am interested. She lifts the dress and shakes it so that the taffeta shimmers across the light. The beads sparkle and dance. Despite my longing, I tell myself that it is too fancy, too expensive for me to buy. A group of women appears. At first, they stand near me. Gradually, they move up to enclose me. They are full of ideas. Together, we lay a plan for how we might purchase the dress, or borrow it, or trade it for something in return. We step toward the dress. Many hands reach past me to caress the beauty of the sparkling bodice and the

swinging skirt. The women agree. This gown is something to wish
for, something to prize, something to take as our own.

I wake from the dream into early morning darkness, my mind expanded by the image of the brilliant colours, the stunning layers of seed bead. I have never owned such a dress. I could not imagine wearing one, and yet a mysterious and inexplicable longing for its shimmery weight follows me everywhere. In the kitchen doing dishes. Walking across the unlikely dusting of autumn snow with dogs bounding behind me. Bent over my desk writing. In the musty basement, folding the endless laundry of two active sons. I want the dress that has appeared so suddenly in my dreams. I want it more than anything else I have ever wanted in my life.

Autumn in this mountain valley is a time when light leaks slowly away. As the Earth tilts farther from the sun, the days grow shorter, the nights longer and longer. The high mountains conspire with the season to increase the impact of the gradual disappearance of light. The sun struggles to reach the valley floor over the tree-crusted ridges that seem to crowd closer as the autumn wanes. Cloud and mist drape the landscape like a shroud. Rain begins to pull the brilliant leaves from deciduous trees, pasting them to the ground. And though an air of foreboding settles in as I make my way through this dark, disappearing world, I am lit from within by the image of the bejeweled bodice. It rises as a bright, glistening possibility, casting fresh light across my life.

After almost two decades of adult womanhood during which I have dressed very plainly – in simple, functional clothes without jewellery or scarves – a lifetime during which I eschewed most feminine, expressive trappings, I am surprised by my strong interest in the sparkly gown. As November darkens, my desire expands beyond the dress – into the realm of vivid colours, gleaming, dangling objects, adornments of many kinds, even the simple application of lipstick. My longing for beauty mingles with even more surprising companions: memories that move forward into my mind, crowding at the loveliness, interrupting the ease and certainty of desire.

In particular, the memories concern my mother and my relationship to her. At first as small and arbitrary as shards of crystal or gold lodged in creek silt, these memories start to become a silty torrent flowing out from the image of the heavily beaded bodice. They re-enter my conscious life as a mother, daughter, sister, wife. Emerging from the dark folds of my past are sharp shots of light that sparkle from gemstones, glisten along the surface of polished shells, gleam against the weight of precious metals and glow in the minute, curved reflections of glass seed beads.

My mother is at the end of stage 6 of Alzheimer's disease (according to neurologist Barry Reisberg's schedule of decline). She has been suffering from the memory-loss illness for years now – perhaps as many as ten, or as few as seven. She can no longer dress herself independently, cook, count or tell time, though she still feeds herself if given time and has a lovely smile. Alzheimer's disease and the related dementias, from the moment they manifest, make the act of remembering day-to-day tasks less and less possible for their victims. In my mother's case, as with millions of others before and after her who have suffered this way, the disease has also robbed her of emotional memories with astonishing thoroughness, turning her own very personal search for lost time into a confused, fruitless pursuit. The disease always infects the power of the conscious mind to remember. It warps memory, weakens it, and finally destroys it.

I ask myself if the dream of the beautiful beaded bodice has prompted memories of my mother to rise in me because she is unable to resurrect many of her own memories anymore. If I have somehow begun to remember what she herself could not, or even, to recall something more universal about being a woman, about living a woman's life. The recollections, though they have begun to dance across my mind much the way anyone's memories might, do not always feel familiar. Do some of these recollections belong to her more than me? Or to her mother? Or to another woman further back in the feminine lineage of my family? Or even to a woman from another age or time altogether? Someone who loved to string necklaces of shell or stone, someone who went to a ball dressed in a beaded bodice the colour of a ripe persimmon, framed by a taffeta skirt as alive as early spring?

I ask myself if memory can be contained exclusively, discretely, in the mind of one person, or if it might be a more collective experience than most of us perceive.

Layers of time build up across a life, obscuring some portions of one's emotional story, exposing others. Perhaps it is inevitable for some memories to secrete themselves into folded corners of the heart. The conscious mind seems to send them there, to banish them from a place of order, control and objective sensory perception. To store them in a place of warmth, rhythm and acceptance, encased by the sound of pulsing blood. These memories of the heart often defy the external significance or insignificance of what happened. They centre more on possibility. Or they cling to loss of opportunity: what never happened, because it couldn't. These are pasts that we all carry, whether we lead eventful lives or not.

Until her illness, though she was a woman of extraordinary talent and ability, my mother led an unremarkable life. I hesitate even to use the word "extraordinary" to describe her, because it might be misleading to those who do not know her. So few of us living on this Earth lead lives of larger purpose, fame or excitement, lives that are measured objectively as "extraordinary." So few of us are renowned. My mother's is one of many day-to-day existences finding their way through time. Nothing special, except to her family. Before she grew ill, my mother expressed her abilities in a modest way, almost without notice to the larger world, much as one small seed of glass rolls around in the palm of a hand. She lived in a grey, stucco-clad bungalow on a quiet California suburban street for most of her married life. She was a homemaker, a mother of four children, keeper of garden, kitchen and hearth. She made no name for herself before anyone other than her family and a few close friends. She met with no great monetary or intellectual successes. She won no awards.

And yet, she was extraordinary. She had a talent, my mother. A talent allowing her to focus on and accomplish anything she set her mind to. One could call it intelligence. Certainly, my mother was gifted with intelligence. But it was more than just intelligence. It was a sort of efficiency combined with competence and focused intention.

She sewed with a neatness and perfection that I have never seen matched. I would watch her, pins held between her teeth, playing with the fabric this way and that, laying it against itself, pressing, stitching. She turned flat lengths of woven, uncut fibre into garments that fit and had form. She did so with speed and confidence. When my brother was restoring a 1956 Chevy sedan in the 1970s, my mother volunteered to reupholster the interior for him. She had never worked with vinyl fabric or sewn a car seat. She figured it out, and the finished product was expert. I watched my mother that summer and decided that she was a magician.

Her competence extended into many areas. Her garden produced prodigious blooms: spunky, bright zinnias lining the back wall of the house, roses opening their musky scent to the dry California air, sweet camellias hanging heavy with spring rain. When she set a table, it was precisely laid out, with a thematic arrangement for the holiday, a crisp tablecloth, polished silver. Everything gleamed with order and intelligence.

As a part-time and on-call teacher, she could master any curriculum set before her, and quickly. She inspired and held the students' respect for her, even those students who came from troubled backgrounds and presented behavioural challenges. They made it to school on days when such a journey may have been next to impossible for them, simply because they knew my mother would notice if they were not there. They knew she cared and they knew her standards had a purpose. She was – and still is – a born teacher. Though now, the lessons she teaches are exclusively those of the heart. Her mind, once sharp and sparkling like a gemstone, has receded and softened. It has grown luminous as a pearl.

The earliest signs of the illness in my mother were not obvious to anyone, including her. A few arbitrary clues began to show themselves in the early '90s, but they are only clear signs viewed through the lens of hindsight. There was a suitcase packed for my father for a two-week holiday that contained a mish-mash of pajamas, sweaters and socks. I dimly recall a car accident during that time, the first ever in my mother's long life as an excellent driver. And a fall from a ladder, sometime before or after the car accident. The fall resulted in a broken leg, the first major physical injury for her, ever, in her sixty-plus years. There may also have been sewing mistakes, coffee pots left on, dinners ruined, cheques not signed. None of her four children are certain when the changes actually began. I was busy at the time with my own baby sons, living a thousand miles away in Vancouver, British Columbia. My older sister was living in the Midwest, having babies of her own. My older brother was following civil engineering jobs from state to state. My younger sister was completing a degree and starting her career. My father, for his part, must have been noticing long before us.

Taken one by one, the first symptoms signaling cognitive failure or systematic memory loss can be excused or explained away as inadvertent, accidental, a whim of mood or a bad day. When families live at a distance from each other as ours does, the gradual, almost imperceptible changes as they register in the beginning are even harder to assemble into a whole. An objective outsider might have difficulty believing that our family had not, by the time our mother entered the third or even fourth stage of the disease, openly acknowledged that something was wrong with her mind. Yet the truth is that the individual mind of a victim and the collective mind of a family will avoid the spectre of loss however it can. Gradually, over time, the tiny, accumulating beads of cognitive memory failure multiply enough that a family's remarkable power to rationalize cannot reduce the changes in behaviour to quirks any longer. The family begins to feel the real weight of the many changes.

To remember is not always a joyful accomplishment, as my mother's illness has taught me. The tragic implications of a woman's memory are told over and over in the story of Demeter and Persephone, a mother goddess and her maiden daughter separated by Hades, god of the underworld, who took

Persephone forcibly as his wife. Demeter pleaded with Zeus to send a messenger to retrieve Persephone, whom she sorely missed. Zeus finally agreed. Hades had no choice but to abide by the wishes of the most powerful god.

Before Persephone left the underworld, Hades offered her six pomegranate seeds to eat. Against her mother's advice, Persephone ate the seeds. These were seeds marked with memory, as it turned out. They embedded in her mind a need to return to Hades for six months each year. The seeds undercut the fullness and permanence of Persephone's reunion with her mother, the reclamation of her innocence. Demeter grieved annually over the loss, a loss of innocence as well as a loss of companionship, a loss of beauty as well as a loss of the daughter. Goddess of harvest, Demeter expressed her multiple layers of sadness in the dying, sagging weight of autumn chill and rain, and then in the still, frozen dormancy of winter. Winter, an annual season of death brought on by the consumption of six polished seeds. Six scarlet beads of truth.

The mother-daughter relationship of Demeter and Persephone expresses the metaphoric power of the cycling of blossom to fruit, death to rebirth, growth toward fruit again. Demeter retained in her mind and heart the memory of a living Earth even in the depths of winter when her daughter was far away. Her daughter, in turn, held on to an annual obligation to descend into darkness and despair, even though she loved her mother deeply. Of course there were the six months when they were together. Demeter's reunion with her daughter's beauty and their delight in companionship allowed the Earth to burst into bloom again, each and every year. Joyous spring, followed by the abundant growth and productivity of summer.

To remember. To return. To give birth to children. This is the cyclical work of memory, of women who do not forget. The

French word *memoire* evolves from the Latin *memoria*, which is closely related to *mourn*. As Persephone and her mother demonstrated, to remember is not always to triumph, or to celebrate. Sometimes it links a person's heart to the underworld of grief. To remember can mean to live with pain or loss beyond imagining, pain that never seems to quit, loss cycling back again and again. To live with this grief daily, trapped by a wall built around the heart. To mourn – for what fate has taken away.

And then, there is that particular form of memory employed by artists who often talk about a "muse," the source of inspiration or creative energy, but we rarely acknowledge its maternal origins. In Greek mythology, the Muses were the nine daughters of Mnemosyne, a powerful female Titan, whose name means, literally, "memory." Memory mated briefly with Zeus and gave birth to the women whom the ancient Greeks believed inspired the creation and study of culture: history, astronomy, tragedy, comedy, dance, epic poetry, love poetry, songs to the gods and lyric poetry. The Muses, with the mothering influence of a recollecting mind, used their talent and beauty to bring art into being. They adorned their society. They opened the hearts and minds of the human beings who felt their presence. They inspired people to express themselves.

Of course I wish that I had written down all the details of my mother's illness, from the first moment I knew something was happening to her until now, nearly ten years later. I should have written down every emotion as it rolled toward me, every act of recompense or healing which has pieced my sorrows together into something that eventually began to resemble a whole again. Instead, I wrote virtually nothing down while it was happening. It was stupid, not to capture the freshness of the impact. Especially since I am a writer, and writers tend to mine their lives for fresh material whenever possible. But the immediacy of feeling, the overwhelming drama which unexpected and chronic illness writes across a life, the uncharted, bushwhacking path which grief always forges – there seemed to be no room for creativity, no breath for desire.

It was as if the Fates, the ancient triple goddess known in Greece as the rulers of time, had stolen my fountain pen from the Muses, who had held it expectantly until then. As if the Fates took the pen in the want and way of these goddesses, descending upon a life in surprise. As if these weavers of destiny clutched the pen firmly to keep me from expressing anything I might wish to say at the time, or ever again. The Fates busied themselves, scribbling furiously across my soul, creating a story that would not be resolved until I had charted, traversed and begun to understand a darkness I did not anticipate.

Now, ironically enough, I must use the power of recollection to find my way through the darkness, to take back the pen as my own, much as Marcel did in Proust's *À Coté de Chez Swann (Swann's Way)*, when he dipped a shell-shaped cookie called a *madeleine* into a steaming cup of tea. This one small event began his long journey across the recollecting mind. I read the first volume of Proust's massive memoir-novel *À la Recherche du Temps Perdu (In Remembrance of Things Past)* in 1982. I was twenty-one years old and living in France on an overseas study program, taking courses in European history, architecture, art history and literature.

For six months, I steeped myself in the beautiful language and culture of Gaul, a place comprised of so many eras of culture and history that the layers cannot all be identified discretely. Gothic or Renaissance churches have foundations dating back to the time of classical antiquity and even further, to a time of Celtic goddess worship at springs that became fountains or wells in churches during the early Christian era. Stained glass that was melted and coloured in medieval times filters modern sunshine through its panes. Modern highways use Roman roads for foundations. Wine *caves* drip ancient mildew off their walls, staining the labels of the newest vintage.

When I lived in France during that winter and spring I was like many twenty-one-year-olds anywhere in the world: energetic, desperate to be in love and trying wildly to grow up. I sat in cafés discussing *Á Coté de Chez Swann* while I sipped *kir* and felt very advanced. Of course, it was easy to focus on memory as an intellectual pursuit. I had little yet to remember about my own life, or the life of anyone else I dearly loved.

Those of us Americans studying overseas who felt intellectually pretentious carried around a copy of Proust in French. Those who wanted to understand its serpentine passages read the English translation, often furtively, as if we were embarrassed to have to do so. I wavered between the two. Our love of Proust's text and others like it that we encountered that year suggested we possessed a deeper knowledge than we were capable of having. We drew on the profound history of the French culture to feel as if our young minds were mature with the wisdom and depth of passing time. Somehow, it seemed that mere contact with this place of history and cultural richness would transform us into sophisticated, astute individuals who understood a great deal and to a great depth. In Proust, we absorbed a superficial knowledge of the power and beauty of memory. Due to our innocence, we overlooked memory's darker side: the prospect of painful revelation, the possibility of loss. Sitting on a smooth, metal *café* chair, watching a crisply attired, always professional *garçon* balance a tray of drinks as he swept past my table, I had no concept then that my obsession with time and memory was a fabricated pursuit driven by the mind, rather than an organic one inspired by the heart.

Twenty years later, it appears that I have been called to unmask the heart, where the most painful and yet also the most joyful experiences reside. Recollection, as my mother and her illness have taught me, is an imperfect mechanism. Memory, sifted through the subjective and sometimes broken sieve of a mind, cannot be tuned, oiled or adjusted finely enough to perform limitless service on demand. Memory can be trapped in the heart, making it an uncertain and unreliable maternal influence. For this reason, memory might be, in the end, a vehicle for truth more than fact, for emotion more than event. Just as one wakes from a dream unable always to recall concrete details of what took place, the mind cannot be counted on to recollect everything perfectly from the past. The mind only remembers what it wishes to, or what the heart can manage at the time.

Those who love someone in the early stages of Alzheimer's disease or the related dementias at some point, either consciously or unconsciously, make the painful connection between the changes taking place and the consequent losses they signal. This is a profound realization that cannot always be reached bravely or openly. Sometimes, it is a completely unconscious acceptance, one made by the heart while at the same time being dismissed or explained away by the mind. At whatever level, change always begets loss and the mind knows it. No desire to *think* about *that,* the mind says. Acknowledging and accepting the realities of any sort of downfall is a challenge. Alzheimer's disease asks for a direct experience of limitation, failure and absence. It requires families and individuals to submit to the scribbling hand of the Fates, to agree that we are flotsam more than a raft on the ocean of our experience. Control the progress of the illness? Not possible. Understand why it happens? More difficult still. Find a cure? Not on the horizon.

The arrival of the Fates – the scribbling heart-openers who are able to see clearly all directions, those carriers of unrequested darkness – inspired in me a mixture of fear, resistance or denial. How could it not? Fear always fights the wind with strong black wings before landing on the limbs of a tree. There it perches, sharp-beaked, a shadow that has momentarily ceased its flight. Below on the ground, Memory and her daughters walk gracefully, with purpose and ease. They find their way steadily, charting a course, staying faithful to the idea that the terrain of loss can always be traversed. It makes sense to follow them.

THE SEED

AUTUMN MOVES toward winter's unforgiving grasp. I watch the high blanket of snow as it drapes lower and lower over the mountains, pulled down further by the cold weather that encases the forests. One morning I wake to see that fresh white snow has fallen so low along the flanks of the mountains that it has nearly reached the shores of the Kootenay River flowing along the valley floor. In the past week, frost and rain have stripped completely the last golden leaves of the birch and alder. The burnished needles of the larch tree have also descended to the ground, leaving behind a grey arabesque of branches that whisper against the evergreen forest, a forest that despite its name has grown silent of any life.

Following the advice of a friend, I have decided to make my dream of the beaded dress real. I want to sew something that might echo the sparkling beauty that has filled my thoughts and stirred an emotional impulse that continues to surprise me in its persistent strength. I realize as I contemplate copying the dress exactly that this makes no sense. I am a mother entering middle age. Where would I wear a formal ball gown of electric green and rich orange, a dress that sparkles and shimmers with Cinderella drama? I am long past the maiden phase of my life.

Although uncertain what to create instead, I do know that it must involve seed beads – tiny spheres of glass collecting themselves across fabric, catching the light. As I child, I strung the small glass beads into necklaces sometimes. I have had no experience with attaching great numbers of tiny beads to fabric, though I know that it can be done.

Seed beads are made from sand or crushed river pebble mixed with plant ash. This mixture is heated to a high degree and formed into long, thin canes. After that, the canes are cut into short sections and the edges of each section smoothed. Originally, seed bead canes were spun and cut by hand with painstaking labour and the beads were considered very precious. As a result of mechanized production, the beads are relatively accessible and inexpensive today.

Skilled craftsmen have made glass beads for thousands of years. By the sixteenth century, Venetian craftsmen and European traders were dominating the manufacture and distribution of seed beads. In sixteenth- and seventeenth-century Milan and Naples, women decorated their clothes with them. They grew so enthusiastic and excessive in their use of the beads that the Senate restricted their use to the decoration of hair ornaments. I often wonder what happened to the illegal beaded gowns – if they were hung at the back of the closet, worn only indoors, or taken apart, bead by bead.

As the Milanese and Napoleon women discovered, the stunning impact of fabric seeded with tiny beads depends on sheer force of number. Each individual bead means so little, possesses almost no value as a common bit of glass cut and smoothed into a tiny sphere with a hole. Yet sewn together into patterns or clusters, the beads form a pregnant array of light and effusive texture. They speak of elaboration and adornment. Of profusion and possibility. They remind me of the moist affirmative uttered by Molly Bloom when Leopold proposed to her on Howth Head in James Joyce's *Ulysses*. She kissed him passionately in reply. Years later, in a stream of consciousness, she recalled the moment:

> ... *yes first I gave him the bit of seedcake out of my mouth and it was leapyear like now yes 16 years ago my God after that long kiss I near lost my breath yes...*

Molly Bloom's yes is one that invites and receives. Her reply is not just an everyday yes, it is a *seedcake* yes, a moist mouthful of pleasure, an offering of nourishment and sweetness, a passing of passion from one tongue to another.

How odd that the dry, unyielding glass beads of my dream could be saying so much to me about prime cause, gestation and moist origins. And yet, how very appropriate. Desire grows from the same root as the creative impulse. A longing for beauty, for abundance, these are one and the same with the urge to express, the compulsion to touch, the instinct to feel expansively and honestly across a canvas, across the surface of a sun-warmed stone, across the skin of another person. My own deepest creative desires – so often unquenched, so frequently unexpressed – have been, for too many years, secured tightly and safely, sealed in a paper envelope like seeds, awaiting the right soil in the right garden to sprout.

One day I wake to find that the rain has shifted to snow. Great, elaborate flakes fall only to disappear as soon as they hit the not yet firmly frozen ground. As I walk downtown to the bead shop, the wind gusts through the cedar trees in the small woodland near our house. The falling snow strikes the dead leaves from a mature horse chestnut tree that litter the ground. The leaves look like so many brown hands, open to receive. The moment the snow lands in these hands, the flakes dissolve.

I stroll around the tiny bead shop, fingering open glass containers of beads large and small, in many shapes and sizes. I explore the wall shelf lined with small vials of seed beads in various colours. I first remember noticing beads as a young girl, when I was about seven or eight years old. I began spending any extra coins I ever had in the bead store, a place called Beadazzled, where I wandered for hours, being dazzled. It had what seemed to me then endless counters of built-in wooden partitions filled with myriad beads: glass, bone, ceramic, plastic and semi-precious stones. They were tubular, round, oval, square, rectangular and free form. They were carved, dyed, spun, sliced and faceted. They were all beautiful to my young eyes. For all their differences, they held in common a place to thread a string or a wire, a way of perforating, in order to hang or attach. The hole drilled in a bead breaks the geometric perfection, but widens the possibilities for use. I delighted in their sparkle, their beauty and their many forms.

My eyes fall on a vial of bugle beads, thin, tubular beads about a centimetre long. They are purplish-blue, mysteriously reflective. I recall a coppery orange fabric I had just admired in the fabric store window on my walk down the main street. The silky fabric was "shot" with threads of the same purple-blue colour. I choose the vial of bugle beads. I find small vials of seed beads in shades of orange that also glisten with a faint rainbow iridescence. I want a third colour and decide on a muted char-coal grey. After I purchase the beads, I walk back to the fabric store, where I greet the owner Maxine and ask to see the fabric displayed in the window. I hold the bolt to the light. Tilted one way, the fabric looks warm – almost bright orange, polished like a new copper pan. Tilted the other way, the fabric casts a faint, purple-blue shadow, one that tarnishes the copper, making it heavy with the ripeness of passing time.

I find a whimsical wrap-around cropped vest in the pattern book. I fuss for a few minutes about whether or not the style of the vest is too "young" for me. But the scale of this vest is small enough that I can imagine decorating it with a pattern of tiny beads. I know that it is a modest substitute for the magnificent dress of my dream. I know that the tarnished orange colour of the fabric is far from the bright persimmon that has so enlivened my thoughts. As I watch Maxine slide her scissors through the fabric shimmering on the cutting table, I reassure myself. This compromise is perhaps all my heart can manage at the time.

When I leave the store with a pattern and the fluttering, autumnal fabric confined to a plain paper bag, I feel tears sting at the back of my eyes, though I am uncertain why. I wipe them quickly away and turn directly into a gust of wind that now carries sleet on its current. I settle my hat more firmly on my head, tuck the bag against my chest and zip my coat to the chin. I carry the coppery fabric home through the dampness, clutching it inside to keep it dry. Later, in the kitchen preparing dinner, I realize the source of the tears. The expressive, impractical fabric I have just purchased is the same colour of a practical cotton fabric that I used in my first major sewing project thirty years ago.

At the age of ten, I had finally sewn enough aprons and potholders to be ready to face armholes and necklines, to stitch a real dress, one I could wear to school, or to church. My first dress was a sleeveless, A-line jumper, an easy project for an experienced seamstress, but one of daunting complexity for my young hands. My mother took me on a special trip to the store to pick out the fabric. I fingered with great longing the voiles and shiny silks, the glistening, fluttering taffetas. I was drawn to their beauty, their nearly weightless drama. My mother steered me away, reminding me firmly that these fabrics were not practical for a beginner. They were too expensive, and would need delicate treatment. They would be difficult to work with, too.

I emerged from the store that day holding a brown paper bag filled with two yards of neatly folded cotton that she called kettlecloth, a sturdy, coppery-orange cotton fabric. *It will wash up well.* My mother said. *And the colour suits your brown hair,* she added on the drive home.

My mother was a thrifty, practical woman. Raised in an unforgiving environment on a remote ranch in central California during the depression and war years, she learned to brace herself against the dust, the heat and the endless worries about whether a crop of grass or a herd of cattle would fail from lack of water. She knew how to make do and how to forestall disappointments. People who live on or close to the land, North American pioneers who have survived economic depressions and droughts, often possess this gritty resolve, this ability to turn away from heartfelt indulgence in order to make a life. *Never choose white fabric, it will show the dirt,* she would say. Or, *no need to line this jacket. Linings are for warmth and function, nothing more.* Her sewing lessons were peppered with sound advice, delivered in a decisive tone.

I often sensed anger hovering behind my mother's decisiveness. This anger may not have been as obvious in reality as it was to my subjective measure. Real or not, it certainly tempered any resistance I might have felt in response to her opinions. Did I openly question the choice of the burnt-orange kettlecloth thirty years ago? I don't recall, but I strongly suspect that I did not. In this and many other circumstances, I feared that to challenge any of my mother's firm and sensible opinions directly might cause the hovering anger I sensed behind her words to dive toward me. This was a clash of wings that I was loathe to experience.

Sewing the simple orange cotton dress many years ago turned out to be a challenge that was almost beyond my young hands and heart. After demonstrating how to lay the tissue pattern pieces on the fabric along the grain line and pin them firmly in place, my mother left me at the dining room table to begin. I slid the scissors across the cotton fabric, cutting one by one the two backs, then the facings for the armholes and neck. I began to cut the final piece, the all-important front of the dress. In my nervousness, I slashed a sizable hole on the fold line of the fabric. I was horrified and distraught. My mother arrived from another part of the house when I called to her in teary desperation. She placed her capable hands on the fabric, assessing the damage. *Maybe we can put an appliqué here*, I remember her saying, *to cover the hole.*

My tears began to subside as I realized that she was not angry. She rummaged in the sewing drawer and found a white daisy with a yellow centre. She placed it on the hole at chest height on the garment and looked toward me. I shook my head reluctantly. I wanted the daisy to be enough of a solution, but knew that it was not. This dress was to be my final 4-H project. It would be judged and scored by master sewing teachers. They would know that the incongruous white daisy at chest height on the orange kettlecloth jumper covered a significant mistake.

My mother knew this too. She rummaged a bit longer in the drawer. Then she turned to me and said: *That's why they put erasers on pencils, Eileen. Everyone makes mistakes. Let's do the right thing.* Though money was never in great supply in my childhood, my mother loaded me into the car and we returned to the store to buy more of the kettlecloth. I felt shame that I had caused this extra expense. I felt gratitude too, for my mother's compassionate understanding that a mistake could be reversed.

It was a warm day in May 1971 when I modeled the finished dress. I posed for my father, who took a photo of me standing awkwardly in the California sunshine in our backyard. Under the sleeveless jumper, I wore a white short-sleeved blouse. I had on white knee socks and a pair of saddle oxfords, functional shoes with brick-red rubber soles that my mother insisted I wear. I had learned to walk late in toddlerhood and needed a brace to support a weakened left leg for a while. The saddle oxfords offered proper support, but they were not at all girlish, fashionable or accepted. While my friends sported platform shoes and canvas sneakers, my feet and legs were not considered sturdy enough. One morning I lost my saddle oxfords before school. This may seem to have been a blessing, but it was a curse. I searched the house for them as my mother grew first worried, then flustered, then angry. I might miss my bus for school. I remember drama, anger and shouting. *For heaven's sake! Where are they? How could you lose your shoes?* Eventually, I found them, hidden under a blanket at the foot of my bed. I made the bus; the crisis was averted. But how could I have lost my shoes?

My mother had been raised in a household afflicted by anger. Though I did not understand this when I was young, her childhood and early adulthood had been strongly shaped by the need to avoid anger or retribution in a family where one or the other could erupt at any time, inspired by abuse of alcohol, or by the rigours and stresses of a hard life. My mother functioned in this environment by learning to do more and better and even more perfectly, to please, and to avoid recrimination. The anger followed her nonetheless into her adult life, sometimes contravening her faith in erasers.

I made sure that the incident of the lost oxford shoes when her anger turned on me was a rare one. I did what I could to avoid it. I made sure that I knew where to find my shoes most of the time and which actions were best and practical for keeping the peace. I often agreed to choices that did not really reflect my truest preference. I overperformed: trying to be the first one ready for church on Sunday morning, the one who never complained, the one who did what she was told. *You had the Midas touch,* my younger sister sometimes says. *You could do no wrong in her eye.* But avoidance of my mother's anger and disappointment did not come without extracting a price. The dissonance between the person I became to conform to her expectations and my true nature created an emotional divide between us. Its quiet presence marked the terrain of my life with a fault line that remained unnoticed for many years.

A week after I purchase the fabric, I find the time one afternoon to cut out the vest. I begin by running a barely warm iron over the iridescent fabric. There are no wrinkles or creases to be noted, but I iron it anyway, thinking about my mother. *Always press your fabric before you begin,* I remember her saying to me that day I began my first major project. I had preshrunk the kettlecloth for the jumper and hung it on the clothesline to dry in the bright California sunshine. It was very wrinkled, as cotton often is once it's washed. *Creases can interrupt the proper lines of the garment. It won't hang right if you lay out your pieces over a crease, and seams might not match up once you do press your finished garment.*

I pin the pattern for the cropped vest to the slippery fabric and slide the scissors back and forth until all the pieces are cut. I unpin the pattern pieces and fiddle with the parts of the vest on the table, getting to know them. Sewing resembles carpentry. The ability to see spatially helps enormously in the assembly of the various parts. I am not very good at this part and were it not for the instruction sheet included with every pattern, I would never get anything right.

I realize as I fiddle that I need to bead the front panels of the vest before I sew them to the lining, so that the thread and knots from beading will be hidden. I tilt and shake the clear containers of seed beads, watching them roll around inside. Then I pour some onto a dish, listening to them tinkle gently against each other when they hit the surface of the porcelain. Outside, beneath the false twilight of a low-lying cloud, a few burnished maple leaves and leathery seed pods still cling to the trees. The leaves and pods mirror precisely the colour of the fabric lying on the table in front of me. I pick up a needle, thread it, and begin. As I experiment with stitching the bits of rounded glass one by one onto the slippery fabric, I am quickly humbled by the task.

The owner of the bead shop had shown me how to attach beads to fabric the day I purchased them. The technique is not really difficult. All it requires is patience. I realize now how small the beads are. The needle I must use for threading them onto the slippery fabric is so long and fine. I fumble with the beads, struggling to arrange them in compact rows. I cannot imagine covering an entire bodice with their shimmer. How long might that take? As the dim afternoon fades, the natural light I always prefer to work by begins to disappear. Dusk settles in and I resort to scattering some of the bugle and seed beads across the fabric in arbitrary clusters of three or four, eager for a rich effect, lacking the ability or the patience. I hear the children coming up the hill after playing outside with friends. I have not started cooking dinner. They will be hungry.

I learn over the next several days that working with seed beads and fabric requires infinite patience, a deep attunement to process rather than outcome, and a willingness to allow very small grains of light to accumulate slowly over time. This must be the true richness of the persimmon-coloured bodice of my dreams. The wealth of something slowly built, the multiplicity of discrete spheres forming a collective impression of sparkling uniformity. On their own, individually, the tiny seed beads bear little weight, make only a small impression. In communion, they can be ornate and somehow more enticing than gold.

It occurs to me as I work with the beads that their glistening appeal might go beyond the visual. I can see already how much patience and investment of selfless labour is involved in beading. Seed beads were eagerly accepted by aboriginal women on their first introduction to the North American continent by Europeans. The Ojibwe, Odawah and Pottawotomi First People called them *Manido-min-esag* or "Little spirit seeds, gift of the Manido." They were and still are revered, treasured and widely used to decorate the ceremonial dresses, pouches, shoes and bags of aboriginal peoples. To fully bead the yoke and upper sleeves of a fine Plains buckskin dance dress takes twenty pounds of seed beads and a year of effort. Aboriginal women understand the spiritual nature of personal time and effort, the precious investment of the little spirit seeds that teach patience and reward with adornment.

I have never had an easy time with adornment. Sliding a bead along the long, thin needle, I recall a girlfriend coming to help me dress up for a high school dance. She brought her make-up bag and curling iron and clothes. After I had dried my hair, she curled it elaborately, then sprayed it to hold its shape.

She applied rouge, mascara, lip gloss and taupe eye shadow to my face. I had never used make-up before that night. I wore a cream-coloured satin granny blouse I borrowed from her, paired with simple, flare-legged velveteen pants my mother had sewn for me. Under the pants, I wore knee-high nylons and platform sandals. I was participating in a ritual of the feminine tribe: the adorning of a young woman, the drawing out of her beauty. The braiding of a maiden's hair, perhaps, or the festooning of her beauty with flowered wreaths.

I was not a comfortable participant in this ritual, nearly as old as societies on this Earth. I did not feel much like myself in the dressy clothing with a face stiffened beneath a canvas of colours other than my own. I never let on to my friend, but I was miserable at the dance that night and of course, was only asked to dance one time. Though I was unaware of it then, I was already well on my way to becoming a functional rather than freely expressive young woman. I continued on that path for years, avoiding the choices I could not bring myself to make. I chose clothes that did not attract attention. I scoffed at the traditionally feminine styles of ruffles, draped silks, high heels and coiffed hair. As a defence, I was more and more inclined to reject completely the "bother" of adornment. I had more important things to do. What I scoffed at and rejected, I now understand, was a deeply buried desire of my own.

My mother was vivid and dramatically beautiful. She had prominent cheekbones, a regal nose, a brilliant smile and dark hair with a lovely wave. She dressed with care and thoughtfulness, choosing styles that were streamlined and practical. Her clothing did not call attention to or enhance her abundant natural beauty. She wore simple, understated costume jewellery matched expertly to her dresses and she applied modest lipstick and light foundation, but little other visible make-up. She kept her hair in a short, easy-to-care-for style. A well-groomed, trim and modest appearance was something my mother valued in herself and wanted for her daughters. She set this standard clearly. She did not encourage loose flamboyance or fussy, elaborate hair or clothing. She was not much for trends either. There was, in my mother's way of adorning, a form of restraint and care that reflected her disciplined nature.

I work on the vest over the course of a few more dim November weeks, fiddling with the beads in the half light, feeling disappointed by the lack of numbers, pressing on despite the troubled memories that the project has stirred. I scale back significantly from my original, ambitious plan to cover the vest in a thick crust of beads. I begin to attach small, arbitrary clusters instead. I build on my first scattering of the beads, arranging in each cluster three long bugle beads radiating from a common centre, one bead each for the body, mind and spirit. In my yoga class once each week, the teacher talks about the union of these three elements of the human experience. I sprinkle the three-part clusters across the vest front and arrange smaller clusters of seed beads around them. What I see before me falls far short of the rich array of beads the dream presented. The colours, though they are tarnished and muted by comparison, nonetheless glisten with an invitation. They catch the light in a pleasing way.

Once I have finished the beadwork, I sew the slippery fabric and lining *right sides together*. As I reverse the pieces, I realize that I have made a big mistake. I have sewn the vest to its lining without first connecting the front panels to the back at the side seams. The finished, lined vest is attached only at the shoulder.

The side seams under the arms flap open like two sets of wings. I survey the outcome of this error, the result of poor concentration on the task, perhaps, or my trademark inability to foresee how the pieces would assemble. Ripping out all the seams and reassembling it is too daunting, given the delicate, slippery nature of the fabric. But the vest is hardly a vest without side seams holding it together.

Standing at the ironing board, I want and need my mother to help me solve this mistake like she did my first project. But I know that her once expert seamstress mind cannot help me now. I tell myself firmly not to cry, not to allow the confusion of losses and emotion to envelop me again.

I remember the leftover bugle beads. I lay the side seams up close to each other, then arrange a handful of the long, tubular beads horizontally in a row like rungs of a ladder, to connect the gap between the front side and the back side of the vest panels. I attach the beading thread to one side of the vest, pass it through a bead and then into the other side of the vest. One by one, I do the same with more bugle beads, until the vest sides are completely attached by the "ladder rung" of beads. The effect is unique, and it solves my problem. After a few more hours of work, I hold the finished product up to admire it. The beading threads are permanently hidden, the scattering of beads attached to the front of the vest as if by magic. Instead of side seams, there are more beads, the bugle beads, slicing the air with their dark sparkle.

Though the vest is modest by comparison to the stunning dress in the dream, I feel a glimmer of pleasure in response to what I have created. I hang the vest in the closet, finished at last.

⚓

In December, I visit my mother before the Christmas holidays. Leaving my young family behind, I drive south out of the mountains to Spokane, Washington, where I board a plane in a landscape bound by ice and snow to travel to the Bay Area of California where my mother lives, near my youngest sister. Since my father died two years ago, I have tried to see my mother more frequently, at least three or four times each year. On these visits, I stay with my younger sister, to whom the task of overseeing my mother's care has fallen.

My sister loves clothes, jewellery and fashion. She always convinces me to shop with her at least once or twice during my weekend visits with my mother. I have been a somewhat reluctant companion. Confident and secure in her own sense of style, as interested in adornment as I never have been, she pulls me into the feminine world of clothing racks, shoe departments and jewellery counters. She suggests that I try things on, or take a risk with colour or style. She holds up a gorgeous silver bracelet and hums with pleasure. She searches to the back of the shelves for her size or mine in a certain colour of shoe. *We have to find them, Eileen. They would be perfect.* She rummages at scarf racks for the best pattern and hue of silk. These are experiences I have almost never had until now, with her.

Look, she calls out to me in the formal wear section of a department store. She is standing beside a sale rack. *Look at these beads! Isn't this fabulous? And look at the price!*

I had not told her about the dream of the bright orange beaded bodice. I had not told her about the month of beading and sewing the copper-coloured vest. I remember the collective of women in my dream, stepping forward to help. I take the dress from her offered hand. In the changing room, I slip it on. The dress is midnight blue, sleeveless and has a mandarin collar. A sparkling constellation of clear and silver glass beads attached by silver threads spreads across the dress front in a pleasing pattern. I feel the weight of the dress as it hangs on my body. Of course a mass of seed beads, made of glass derived from fused sand, would be heavy.

Standing in the harsh light of the changing cubicle, I decide with great disappointment that I don't like the dress. I hear a voice within me, rationalizing, disputing. *But it is such a good price, and it has the beads I have been longing for.* Another part of me is not fooled. The blue-black velvet fabric pales my winter skin in an unattractive way. Something about the colour makes more noticeable the grey streaks in my once dark brown hair. And though the dress should be floor length, my long legs cause it to brush against the top of my ankles. This, I know, is not the gown of my dream, the one I never tried on. That gown had no weight, only beauty.

I realize that I cannot turn to the material world to call up the feeling the gown of my dreams has given me – a feeling that every life, every heart, has the potential to be a beautiful bead, fully rounded with potential, colourful, gleaming and filled with light. Removing the dress, I take a small but important mental step away from the cramped and critical evaluation of how I look. I place the dress on the hanger. As I leave the changing room, my sister looks at me expectantly. I mumble a few words about the dress being too short and the wrong colour and place it back on the rack. Together, we wander off to the next store. *You always have to try,* my sister says reassuringly. *How else would you ever know?*

The vest hanging in my closet back in Canada, even from this distance, has awakened in me a search for the seedcake yes, for a heart that receives the wisdom of a mother's love to become a whole being who can embrace desire. I feel myself move one step further, beyond the range of intellect, to other aspects of my self previously out of reach. On the drive home from Spokane a few days later, I know that as much as I am moving north along Highway 2 into the mountains, so, too, am I setting out on an internal search to explore more deeply the possibility that the dress of my dreams had very little to do with beauty of the material kind.

MOTHER SHELL

BY EARLY JANUARY, the winter world outside has gone completely still. Other than a handful of chickadees who venture daily to a feeder I have suspended in an old apple tree, and the odd raven etching its black form against the snow-white sky, the birds have disappeared. I cannot see or hear the merlin hawk who hunts along the slope in spring and summer, or the finches who like to decorate the trees with their chatter as they pass here or there.

Flakes of snow fall in great heaps on the dormant landscape, settling and smoothing out the rough edges of rock and the scruffy forests on the steep mountain slope across the river that I watch from my studio window. In Taoist philosophy, the *yin* energy that dominates in winter is defined as essentially feminine. Taoists associate yin with shade, cold, contraction, water, inactivity, the moon and earthly matter. In winter, their definition of yin reigns over the landscape like an ice queen as the sunlit, productive, masculine world retreats behind a cold curtain of dormancy. True to the season, I feel an increasing pull toward the diffused light of the moon.

One day, when I am searching my sewing basket for a needle and thread, I come across a small tin box with a hinged lid. This container once belonged to my husband's grandmother, Constance Blytha Copeman Pearkes. It was the place where she stored buttons – those she had cut off worn-out dress shirts, or others worth saving that she had pulled from clothes destined to become rags. Button boxes and jars were once common in households, especially when sewing was a basic domestic skill possessed by most women. A button box or jar was the first place to look if a lost fastener needed replacing. As a child, I sometimes played with the buttons in my mother's button jar, lining them up and sorting them by colour or shape. Whenever I sewed something for dolls or myself, my mother checked the jar for possibilities before we headed out to the fabric store to purchase new ones.

Blytha Pearkes was, like my mother, a thrifty, practical woman. A peer of my mother's mother, she was born in 1903 at home on a farm in the Bow River valley, outside Cochrane, Alberta. Her early years were, like my mother's and my grandmother's, informed by isolation. It was perhaps this isolation that taught Blytha about making do, about the value of saving any small button or length of yarn or thread for a future use. When she died, the small metal box containing fifty or more years of accumulated thrift and its associated clothing history was passed to me.

Inside the box on top of the piles of buttons lies a makeshift string of several dozen shell shirt buttons threaded together and tied into a loop. They have been organized into two groups: those buttons with four holes and those with two. I imagine Blytha clipping them off the worn-out shirts and patiently stringing them together for a future use, marveling at her legendary organizational talents and thrift as I finger the string. These buttons saved decades ago now have collector value beyond their intrinsic worth. Until the mid-twentieth century, shell buttons were common on clothing. In the Mississippi River watershed, entire towns built up around the freshwater mussel fishery that provided shell for nearby button factories. The exhaustion of the mussel supply in the Mississippi valley, combined with the development of plastics, changed the way buttons were made in the postwar period. Today, shell buttons are much more precious than they once were.

In *The Universal Bead,* Joan Erikson describes another, long-ago use for shell that invested great value in the otherwise common material. Aboriginal people on the eastern side of North America made beads by hand out of purple and white clamshells. Hours of patient honing and drilling resulted in little tubular beads. These beads are called *wampum,* and some are very old, much older than European presence on this continent. The Haudenosee (Iroquois) strung the wampum beads as a record of treaties, or to mark the performance of sacred ceremonies and songs. They treated their precious chains or belts of shell with the same great respect accorded all agreements and promises in their culture. Europeans noticed the high value the Haudenosee gave the wampum and mistook it as a form of monetary currency. According to the Haudenosee, however, the value of the shells was not one of material wealth but of the promises they represented, whether to another tribe, or to a higher power.

Around the world, indigenous cultures have always valued all sorts of shell beads. Erickson also describes a European explorer travelling deep into the Congo who recorded that the indigenous people there called the shell beads that had travelled in from the coast of Africa "God's children." To those who lived near the ocean, shell beads must have seemed like strings of shattered moonlight glowing on the surface of a hand.

The First People on the northwest coast of North America also considered shells more than just common objects. They gently raked the sand over and over, for hour upon hour when the tides were out, to harvest *dentalia*, tiny, conical mollusks of beauty and delicacy that they valued much as the Haudenosee valued wampum. Dentalia have been found in archeological digs all over the interior plateau of the northwest, emerging from some of the driest soil imaginable, recording the widespread trade routes that existed between tribes. The dentalia were also used as ornaments, sometimes stitched onto Coast Salish wedding bonnets, row after row as a reflection of the bride's value. Northwest native tribes also adorned clothing with a type of northern abalone growing in the coastal waters, the iridescent inner shell esteemed for its magical rainbow colours.

Some of the shell buttons in the box still have remnants of the outside surface of the shell on one side, evidence of the rough exterior that was not completely smoothed away when the button was made. Shells often present a turbulent exterior texture that belies an interior of polished calm. Sometimes when visiting the ocean, I'll find an empty oyster shell lying on the sand and pick it up, running my hands over the smooth, luminous lining. I'll cup my palm around the shell's rough outer sphere, thinking of the inside as a concave form of moon compressed into the shell's curve.

The ocean, a body of water – *la mer* in French, a word so closely related to the word for mother, *la mère*. The ocean honours the moon's tidal work with these shells washed up from the salty deep. In the most glistening form, the inner lining of shell is called mother-of-pearl, the container that cradles and nurtures the pearl itself. It is the oyster's work, the moon's work, a woman's gift to the world. On the reverse side of the rough exterior which life often presents, spreads a smooth protective vessel, a surface that gives rise to something of great feminine beauty.

My younger sister recently found a photo of my parents when she was cleaning out files in the family home. I had never seen this photo when I was growing up. The camera caught my parents as they left the reception on their wedding day. Mom is vividly, naturally beautiful – dressed in an elegant dark suit, fitted at her slim waist, narrow around her long, shapely calves. She wears a single strand of pearls and a white skullcap hat trimmed with a wisp of netting. In one properly gloved hand, she tightly clasps a woven handbag shaped like a small treasure chest. The other hand stretches behind her, grasping for my father, who appears more than willing to have his hand in hers. He wears a suit that seems two sizes too big. In his hand swings a small, rectangular overnight bag. His face is beaming, his smile loose and full of joy. As they leave the reception, my parents clearly have places to go, things to do in this life. They are both full of hope, and it appears that my mother will lead the charge. *Hurry up, Dave*, her trim, attractive figure seems to be saying as she moves in advance of him. *Let's go.*

All her life, my mother did not wait for things to come to her. She left her rural home to go to university several hours by train away, the only child in her family to do so. She never returned to what she thought of as a dusty, hot and drought-troubled ranch, even if, after the depression and war years passed, it became more and more prosperous. She left home again metaphorically when she married my father and established a life with him. In him, she chose a creative and joyful man, the antithesis in some ways of her brusque, ambitious and physically hard-working father. She made sure we had a stable, loving home to grow up in and she urged us all to complete higher education. I can recall her more than once pressing my father to stick with a job when he felt like moving on or changing roles. Where my mother was, focused action and self-discipline were never far behind.

As the effects of our mother's Alzheimer's became more and more noticeable to her family, her lifelong decisiveness began to diffuse. She assumed the role of follower more than leader. This change rocked the foundation of our family. Oddly enough, in the early stages of the illness, her lost abilities originally felt more like choices she had made to cease to do something. The concept of free will and action so dominates our culture's understanding of human experience – and determination and decisiveness so defined my own mother's personality – that it took our family a long time to realize that she was not choosing to cease to do things, that instead she was a passive victim of an illness gradually taking hold of her mind. Of course, no matter how slowly and gradually Alzheimer's advances, the process always, every step of the way, robs *all* its victims of a choice. This is when the courage of a family must assert itself. If it does not, a disease of relentless loss such as Alzheimer's will shrink every soul it encounters.

Who steps up willingly to embrace the slow, gradual departure of a loved one as she has always been known? Who rushes to admit the onset of limitations that will progress and progress and progress until only the shadow of a personality remains? The early effects of this illness are far too minute to be easily and suddenly accepted with a horrible flash of recognition as the results of a biopsy can be, or a traumatic heart attack. There is no panic-stricken moment, no focused drama in a diagnosis. An illness such as my mother's, a passage out of the mind and body so slow and gradual as to be almost unseen in the first stages, has few equals for its pace, its ambiguity, its near absence of treatment options or its bleak certainty in outcome.

In the mid-'90s, my parents came north to Vancouver to help me recover from an illness and surgery. It was then that I first saw plainly enough what I could no longer deny or dismiss: that the changes in my mother were not a matter of her personal choice. I had been feeling tired and unwell for over a year prior to that and experiencing more and more pain in my monthly cycles. At a check-up, my doctor had discovered a fibroid tumour the size of a cantaloupe melon embedded in the wall of my uterus. It was large enough and had wreaked enough havoc in my body by the time it was discovered that I was anemic and in significant pain. Removing the tumour meant having what Western medicine terms a "partial hysterectomy," the removal of the womb and cervix but not the ovaries. I have never understood why this procedure is called a "partial" hysterectomy. It felt then the same way it does now: like a whole loss, not a partial one.

Hysterectomies are common procedures. Many women have them in response to "gynecological complaints" or cancer. I knew that the solution to my illness was medically safe and logical, considering the fact that I was chronically anemic, in considerable pain and completely exhausted. I will admit to feeling horror and revulsion at the invasiveness of the tumour, an unnatural growth that I wanted to have removed so that I could again be well. I turned to surgery as a solution, though I now understand that the surgery turned out to be the start – not the end – of the healing process.

I had an impulse when I realized that I would have to have surgery and recover from it while caring for two small children. I wanted my mother near me. I needed her help.

I was not aware then that my mother was probably between stages 2 and 3 of Dr. Barry Reisberg's schedule of declines. This stage is a relatively early moment in the eternity of the illness, one in which cognitive disabilities begin to register undeniably. The lack of much contact I had had with my parents over the previous two years compounded the surprise I experienced when my mother arrived with my father. Overwhelmed by my own struggle to heal physically and resume the consuming work of a young family, I was unprepared for the version of her that greeted me that week. She lost grocery money, could not find the hospital or cook dinner. When I asked her to do laundry, she shrank several fine cotton dress shirts. She was unable to help much with the children. She seemed very distracted and even withdrawn. As I struggled from my bed to the bathroom and in and out of the kitchen to do the few chores I could manage, I began to grope with the possibility that something might be terribly wrong.

But compassion for my mother was not my first response. I was, more than anything, angry. I even felt betrayed and enormously let down. Could it be that I was unable to depend on my own mother? Could it be that she would not *do* anything to help me heal? I was also confused. This fed my resentment. My mother was there. She was present as she always had been. She was in the room. She had not died. She had not chosen to stay home. She had willingly come north to be with me. She seemed on the surface of things like a parent I could depend on. But the absence of her actual, practical support, guidance and competent energy at a time when I so needed it spoke a lesson that has taken many years for me to understand.

Looking back, that visit from her was the moment when loss began, with compounding finality, to expose my lifelong spiritual weaknesses like a *bas relief*, showing me clearly how and in which ways I needed to grow and be stronger if I was to become whole. The initial losses in my mother's functioning as caregiver and homemaker were to prove small and almost inconsequential by comparison to the many losses still to come. Unlike in the world of finance, the first losses in a dementia are not the best. They involved a change not only in a mother's way of caring for her children and husband, but also in expressing her love toward us. They began a long, painful process, as she slipped ever so gradually from one who does, to one who simply is, to one who has been. Beginnings are not always full of hope. They can be wrenching. And they can inspire resistance.

Searching further in the small metal box, I find another, smaller string of shirt buttons. All of these have two holes. I carefully sort the pile of single buttons jumbled together in the box, searching through the metal and plastic and bone of various sizes and colours for anything made of shell. I locate at least a few dozen in various sizes and tones. Some of them have the grey-blue luminosity of mussel, some are pearly white, some are ecru, perhaps stained by time. Sitting with the box on my lap I feel an urge rising in me to make something marked by these buttons. I want to pull the moon toward me, to allow the cool, reflective rays of its light to enter my life.

The largest shell button is nearly four centimetres in diameter, the colour of cream and smooth as glass. A real beauty, probably used on a coat, or another thick woolen garment. Its soft radiance reminds me of a ceremonial button blanket I once saw hanging in the Museum of Anthropology in Vancouver. Button blankets are post-European contact regalia worn at feasts by members of Pacific Northwest tribes: the Haida, Tsimshian,

Tlingit, Nuxalk, Kwakiutl and Nisga'a. Doreen Jensen, a Gitxsan artist, calls button blankets "totem poles on cloth." They indicate family and tribal affiliations, as well as personal power. The one on display in the museum was made of wool the colour of the night sky, appliquéd with traditional designs the colour of a woman's blood. The buttons attached along the horizon of the wool symbolize peace, spirituality, harmony and balance. The dark wool has the ability to make the wearer invincible and the red wool signifies supernatural power.

Australian aboriginals, ancient Sumerians, Hindus, Normans, Celts, American aboriginals, Taoists – all made reference to the mystery of menses and imported reverence for the creative rhythm into their belief systems. In ancient Greece, menstrual blood was known as supernatural red wine given to the gods by Hera when she was in her virgin form as Hebe prior to her marriage to Zeus. Many cultures throughout time and around the world have believed that the woman's ability to shed blood monthly without dying signaled in her a sort of supernatural power. They invested magical properties in blood, especially menstrual blood, a mysterious capacity that was at once inexplicable and revered. Frequently, cultures directly related the regular passage of blood from a woman's body to the rhythm of the cosmos, most specifically to the cycling moon, a heavenly body that so resembles the small circles of shell attached to the woolen blankets.

Shell buttons came to aboriginal cultures of the northwest through the fur trade. Manufactured in the Philippines and elsewhere for the trade in the eighteenth and nineteenth centuries, the shell buttons were highly prized by aboriginal women from the moment they arrived, as were the woolen blankets brought by the Hudson's Bay and other companies. Women began to use the shell buttons to trim and emphasize appliquéd images of raven, killer whale, eagle, wolf or other marks of the family crest. A button blanket can contain hundreds of shell buttons assembled into patterns. These buttons may have, according to contemporary tribal elders, originally symbolized the many souls who form the family lineage represented by the crest.

I remember standing in the museum, mesmerized by the tiny buttons, glowing like small moons against the dark horizon of fabric. They felt like souls, now that I think about it. There was something about the combination of navy blue or black and red wool, something about the row after row of gleaming moons and the careful stitching done by women that made me wish for the rest of the day and into the night that I could have fallen asleep wrapped in the blanket's ceremonial warmth. I could not articulate then what now seems to me a desire to be surrounded by the supernatural rhythms of the night sky, the flow of magical blood and the light of a glowing moon.

I believed for a long time that women were tied down by blood, that we were wrapped tightly and often against our will in the dark cycles of the moon. My first monthly period came early, at the age of eleven and a half. Inclined to be a tomboy, I was still playing basketball and football on the playground at recess. In 1973, I was more likely to want to stay in the classroom at lunch with a large group of boys to listen to the World Series on the radio than I was to cluster with a group of girls near the hop-scotch patterns painted on the asphalt. I can remember begging the teacher for just that privilege one year, so that we could listen as the legendary Swingin' A's made it all the way to the top.

The arrival of my monthly cycle during this time felt like an interruption to my freedom, an imposition on my prefer-ences. It did not seem fair to me that girls had this bother and boys did not. This sense of unfairness about what other cultures throughout history have deemed a mysterious source of power continued as I matured. I resisted my role as carrier of blood. I felt it was unfair that women's careers had to be interrupted by childbirth, and men's did not. That women bore the worry about pregnancy, and men did not.

It never occurred to me to consider a woman's monthly cycle as something potent, a reflection of the capacity not only for magic but also for an ability to contain and hold human life, joy and grief. Last year, I encountered an archeologist's description of a grave belonging to the Sinixt Interior Salish, also known as the Arrow Lakes Indians. The grave held two tiny bodies: a seven-month fetus and a two-year-old toddler, both of whom probably died in a smallpox or measles epidemic sometime in the late eighteenth or early nineteenth century. When diggers exposed the grave, they found hundreds of dentalia shells buried with the babies, as well as copper beads and buttons acquired from trade with Europeans. The precious items had been scattered across the surface of the skeletons, mixed in with the riverbank gravel where the bodies had been placed in their shifting tomb. I try to imagine the mother of these children, whose dark, enclosed womb gave rise to the blood of life and then expelled the blood of death. Was it possible for her soul's shell to contain the far reaches of this sadness? How she must have suffered! How her hands must have trembled as she helped scatter the precious bits of shell, metal and glass over the bloodied pearl from her womb.

Sitting with the weight of Blytha Copeman Pearkes' old button box pressed into my lap, I recall a day I visited her many years ago, before my own children were born. When I arrived in the apartment where she lived alone after her husband's death, I found her uncharacteristically quiet and brooding. She was typically an optimistic woman, prone to repeating jokes, making quips and keeping things light. I sat beside her and asked her if everything was all right. *Today would have been Pep's sixty-third birthday,* she said to me, her eyes misty with sadness. I knew only faintly that she once had a daughter who died at the age of seven. I said I was sorry, then listened as Blytha explained her daughter's illness and death. Fifty-six years later, her loss seemed to be as fresh as if it had happened the day before. Blytha was not one to wear her sorrow on her sleeve, but I realized then that she contained this tragic loss within her all the same.

I search all four corners of her button box to find every single shell button it contains. I count several dozen of the little shirt buttons and nearly two dozen of the larger shell buttons in various shapes and sizes. I know that there is not enough here to make a button blanket like the one I remember. I doubt I would have the patience. How can I bring these small moons into my life to adorn the dark days of winter with the female lineage of my family? Visual artist Jessie King once sewed 365 tiny shell buttons around the base of her wedding dress. I have about one tenth of the amount, and I am not getting married. Another version of King's idea surfaces. I will sew a long, swinging skirt with a hemline marked by a marching row of moons. Buttons brought back into the light from the dark corners of a tin box.

I rummage in my fabric cupboard and find a length of red wool, originally intended for another project long since abandoned. The wool is lightweight and soft. I cut out a simple, un-lined A-line skirt. Though it takes a few days to get the fit right on the rim of my hips, I have finished sewing the skirt in less than a week. I press and hem the bottom so that it falls to just above my ankles. After that, I arrange the buttons I have chosen, mixing up the sizes – some larger, some smaller – in an even row near the bottom edge of the skirt. I thread a needle with bright red thread and fasten each one securely. A few days later, when the skies clear, I set out for a walk dressed in my new skirt. The weight and warmth of the wool swings around the tops of my red leather boots. When I try to take brisk, expansive strides through the cold, the buttons click hard against each other. I worry that they might split apart, so I slow down. The clicking of shell softens. It seems to be important, on this brilliantly sunny midwinter day, to take more time, to ease into the gentle rhythm of my own true nature.

⚜

By the time I had recovered physically from my surgery, the situation I called my life had worsened to the point that avoiding mental and spiritual reconstruction had become impossible. My mother's inability to provide me with support during this time had felt like an act of further betrayal. But of course it was not. Her lack of mental presence that week and in the months and years after was a clear, carved message. Seen now through the scaffold of memory, my mother was offering me wisdom and understanding: if I wished to end personal dissatisfaction, I would have to turn inward to find my way. No one could really do the work for me, even her. Only my heart's strength could bring me along a path toward wholeness. The path would be marked by suffering, self-examination and acknowledgment. And it would wind its way through the expansive forest of her illness.

It is possible that the physical place of the womb is the extent of a woman's ability to form a protective shell. It is also possible that the womb is only a physical symbol of the essential feminine work of nurturing and protecting, of holding and containing. It took losing my own womb to point me painfully toward the latent cultural value of this portion of the female body and the work it represents, with its cyclical strength and its ability to contain new life through blood and expansion.

The very nature of loss is that as soon as something significant is taken away, what remains is the shape of the work needing to be done, the sculpted pattern of one's path toward wholeness. Transformation does not take place without a letting go, a relinquishment of one thing for another, one state of being for another, one attachment for another. Transformation is not always a willing and cheerful change from an outgrown way to a chosen result. Transformation can thrust its demands upon us, while we fight against it, unawares. It was hard to imagine then what I now know could be true – that loss might result in an opportunity for wholeness, that blood can be both a burden and a source of life.

My mother slowly lost the capacity to run a household and then her inabilities spread to self-care. In just a few years after their visit, she was unable to accomplish even relatively simple tasks such as washing her hair or clothes. She began to be afraid of bathing, and she could no longer cook meals. She grew quiet and inactive. She showed fewer and fewer preferences of any kind, turning to my father to know what to order in a restaurant or which dress to choose off the rack. In all the facets of her daily life, she began to wait more than act, to listen more than talk, to receive more than give. The effects on her husband and her children were profound. My father, who had followed her out of the church with arms swinging freely and a grin as wide as the prairies, was without his leader. My mother, in turn, was losing the protective coating of self-discipline and resolve that she had worn most of her life. Her perfectionism, strong focus and successful drive to construct a beautiful life for her children, all of this was dissipating into something that looked like profound fatigue.

We began urging our father more and more to do something. He was slow to act and we as her children showed impatience at his inability to do so. This was hardly fair to him, a man who never bathed a baby or tended a sick child. After over four decades of being married to a woman of action, how could he be expected to take over her care with any ease or grace? Though we could not see it at the time, our mother's failings were demanding of all of us that we alter the way we cared about her. This required us to expand our emotional horizons. Bluntly put, we needed to begin to mother our own mother.

Issues surrounding aging and illness always ask for expansion of the heart, but the human response is often contraction. My father was too tired, too established in his own life habits to be able to shift the dynamic significantly between the two of them. So, while he gradually took over the cooking, shopping and laundry, he could not bathe my mother or help her dress. He took her any way she came: dressed in clean or dirty clothes, hair cut and shaped or greasy and unkempt. He loved her steadily, consistently, through it all. In this way I am certain he offered her heart comfort as the illness progressed. I am certain he helped her maintain emotional dignity. I am certain he eased her pain.

Charting a path back across the memories, I can see that the painful truth of my mother's condition arose finally and honestly in our family only when she ceased to be able to care for and nurture herself physically. All the preceding lapses over the first five or six years of her illness that had puzzled and concerned us touched on how she cared for other people or possessions: her husband, her children, her grandchildren, her workplace or her household. Somehow, these lapses were more excusable and easily rationalized. But when our mother could no longer easily bathe herself, launder her clothes or dress neatly, her illness became undeniable.

One day a few years ago, I helped my mother bathe and dress. I ran the water carefully and guided her very slowly into the tub that she had become afraid of. I settled her into the water and soaped her body, remarking at the smooth and almost new feel of the skin on her back. She sighed with pleasure. *That's nice and warm*, she said, when I scooped water onto her skin to rinse the soap. I found myself calling on powers of empathy I did not know I had, speaking softly and reassuringly to her about the safe feel of the tub's curved shape. Throughout the process, I marveled at her increasing compliance, her deep willingness to receive care and love. Her dependence was being finally and vividly exposed by an illness that has no cure.

While I bathed her, the vulnerability of mother and child was exchanged one for the other. I became in a small handful of moments the protective caregiver to a woman who had once cared for me. Something about the experience led me to think about how I had been caring for myself, both before and after my own illness and surgery, about how I had been caring for our two children since their birth. I knew I was not just bathing my mother but that she, through her illness, was offering me a gift as well. Had I been gently mothering the deepest aspects of my own being? Had I been the most compassionate mother I could be to my children? Was I a mother who protected them adequately to help them evolve into strong, individual beings? I began to wonder if my own nurturing work had been missing a key element: a receptivity, a gentleness. A passivity and a quiet love. Inclusive compassion and nonjudgemental respect. The light of the moon.

As I lifted my mother from the bath and toweled her off while she shivered on the bath mat, I felt a wave of gratitude. It was a turning point not only in my willingness to offer practical assistance to the family, but also in my larger understanding of the art of nurturing. Nurturing is an essential human activity. Whether men or women perform nurturing tasks, the spirit of the task must suspend in good balance between the active and the passive. Those who nurture best are generous and receptive, thorough and flexible.

Babies possess an inviting helplessness. Most mothers have a deep instinct to protect and care for infants. The infant's vulnerability prompts a biological response in a woman, one that is informed by the heart. Our present culture does not greet increased helplessness in an aging elder with the same energy and awe. Helplessness in an elder is a repulsive thing we see only as a sad loss of capacity. Something to stow shamefully away out of sight in an extended-care facility. Something to avoid at all costs. Something it would be better not to dwell on. I have grown used to the reactions of friends: their pity for my family's situation laced with relief that their own parents are not suffering this way. They try to hide the relief, but I hear it in their voices. It is a sign of our times, this relief. A sign that the unpleasant and shameful aspects of aging have been avoided, at least for a time.

In the crisis of my mother's prematurely decreasing independence, I can see a larger cultural commentary on dependence. Why would my elder's dependence frighten me so? What about it makes me shrink back with horror or denial? Why is it considered an unrealistic burden to care for my increasingly dependent mother? Does one's own experiences as a nurtured being determine the capacity to care for *anyone* who is vulnerable, despite age or circumstance? In Alzheimer's disease and the related dementias, families encounter the truly cyclical nature of care: those who once cared for us must now be cared for by us. Their needs are great, immediate and childlike. They take us by surprise.

A few days after my first clicking walk in the red button skirt, I wake deep in the night, a regular habit of mine. Wandering around the main floor of the house, I step to the window, where I see a new moon rising quietly in the dark sky, poised above the winter-white world. A sphere of deadened dust and rock, the moon turns and orbits Earth daily, usually unnoticed, always receptive and cool. I can go for days or even weeks without measuring its unassuming light against the skin on my forearm, or watching its curve echo the fathomless arc of the night sky. Tonight, I see it floating in the indigo darkness as if for the first time: a sickle of light set off against an eternity that can only be imagined.

Blood comes and goes like the moon, washed by the tides of a womb, a protective vessel, a container that hosts and shapes human life, then brings it into the world.

The feminine rhythms of a song hummed under one's breath, the circling of a spoon around the edge of a pot, the heel of a hand gently kneading bread. Rhythms that speak with certainty that the task of that moment can find a position at the reflective centre of a woman's world. Was it simply that my mother had too many tasks to complete in the day that she could not slow down and expand gently into the actual process of care? Or was my mother part of a more universal and cultural struggle to value nurturing work, prompted by rejections of the value of homekeeping as the second wave of feminism rose in the '70s? It is possible that I felt this divide more than she did. Either way, as Carol Lee Flinders points out in *At the Root of this Longing*, the personal and the collective experiences of women are more entwined than one might assume. This relationship between the individual biography of a woman and the trends of the culture in which a woman lives, works and loves fuzzes the lines between an event, its origins and its outcome.

Alzheimer's disease has wrenched from me in an untimely and even cruel way a chance of a long adult relationship with the woman who gave birth to me, the woman who taught me to sew, cook, clean and create a home. The woman who taught me to love and invested in me the courage to face adversity. The nurturing of my children has been heavily shadowed by the contemporary losses in my own lineage of women – my health difficulties that resulted in the loss of my womb and my mother's slow parting from this world. My work as a woman is shadowed by a realization that my mother will not pridefully watch me take care of my children. She will not offer me loving advice or even take up their care occasionally herself. Nor will she share her life stories with them, or taste with pride my version of the pie she taught me to make. I can see her, standing at the counter in the kitchen, showing me how to "feel" whether the crust had the right proportion of shortening and flour. I can see her rolling the dough out expertly on a floured fabric pastry frame stretched tight by a system of wood slats and metal rods. I can smell the cinnamon-sugar dusting she put on the scraps of dough, to be baked as small cookies for her children to nibble on.

The losses I describe are not unique to my family, or to me. They are merely emblematic of what is suffered by so many of us, inner wounds we experience that lead to physical, psychological and spiritual illness. These losses are connected through the heart to the losses experienced many, many years ago by the women of my family: my mother, my mother's mother, her mother, and perhaps even before that, by women from the maternal line whom I cannot even name.

The lining inside an oyster shell is like the moon. It does not take a stain. Blood runs freely off the polished nacre, the smooth inner surface. It inspires me, the mother-of-pearl. As a shell of protection, a bleached husk formed within the great swelling rhythms of the sea. And though I no longer have a husk within me, I do have a heart. The heart, like the womb, has the capacity to circulate blood, to expand and to compassionately nurture a life.

Learning to care for my mother as she has succumbed increasingly to Alzheimer's disease, even briefly during my very occasional visits from a long distance away, has been an experience of inestimable value. Sponging the soft skin on her back, holding a spoon to her mouth, stroking her cheek with love – these small acts, offered infrequently but always with the most presence I can muster, are teaching me how to nurture truly, from the deepest and most loving aspect of my feminine being. These offerings allow me to bring the presence and care of my loved one to the centre of my world. I recognize an earlier reluctance, and am beginning to allow a quiet, receptive energy to bloom in my life. I am reminded to take full responsibility for nurturing both the natural world I live in and the children I helped to create.

The feminine aspect of nature often manifests itself as a passive presence: the gentle unfolding of a blossom's petals, the malleable, adaptive flow of water over rocks, the cool, approachable light of the Earth's rotating satellite. Here is a gentleness and protection that allows potential to emerge in its own time, not to be stifled. No one can stare at the sun for even a moment, yet the moon's safe and luminous light can be gazed at for hours. My mother, more and more a creature of the moon as her illness has progressed, offers me great feminine wisdom as she slowly departs from this world. In the opening of her defensive glass shell that Alzheimer's disease has brought about, in the final exposure of her vulnerability, in the unmasking of her well-practised independence, efficiency and self-sufficiency, I have found a priceless, healing gift.

There can be a searing power in compliance, a vivid beauty in reflection and a paradoxical warmth in light cast back twice from its source. The message from the wampum and from my mother's illness – it is a pure one. That we love ourselves and those who need us in our world. That we protect them as fiercely and yet as generously and compassionately as we can, with shells of great smoothness on the inside, with a nacre that surrounds closely while offering plenty of room to grow. That we begin our nurturing of others by taking care of who we really are as individuals, so that we can allow the light of the moon to radiate outward into the troubled world. This, I have realized, is the mother-of-pearl.

THE MENDING HAND

IN AN UNTIMELY WAY, a favourite pair of thick woolen socks has thinned at the heel and opened at the toe. As the wind howls and the snow deepens outside, I want the socks to keep my feet warm. Tendrils of mist rise up off the steel-grey lake. Stiff winds tear at a Christmas wreath still hanging on the front door. The gaiety and décor of the holiday season have long since passed. In the severe cold, the branches of evergreen have turned blackish-green. The heater hums nearly constantly in the house. In my studio, water left in a glass freezes into a brick of ice overnight. It takes nearly an hour to warm the air enough so that I can write.

I never wore woolen socks as a child in California, other than a few times when I skied or hiked in the Sierra Nevada Mountains. It's taken me awhile to get into the habit of keeping my feet warm in these mountains. I have a particular fondness for thick woolen socks, especially these, of the hand-knit variety. The socks float around the laundry room for several days. I am reluctant to stuff them into the rag bag I keep in the kitchen closet. I decide I will try to repair them.

From Thimble to Gown by Ethel Van Gilder is a depression-era manual on the art of sewing and mending. Published the year after my mother was born, it discusses many types of construction problems and their solutions. In Chapter III, under the subheading Mending, Van Gilder talks about darning. Darning is a type of hand sewing that weaves thread or yarn in two directions to fill in a hole that has worked open in a sock or in cloth. According to Van Gilder, darning can also close many other types of gaps, including straight, diagonal and three-cornered tears. But in particular, darning serves well to mend holes. Of course, a hole can be closed up again without the intricate work of darning. The arcs of the open gap can be drawn together to meet as a straight edge and sewn up quickly with a needle and thread. This method of joining two sides of a circle into a straight line, as anyone knows who has tried it, results in puckering. Van Gilder does not subscribe to puckering. No well-trained seamstress would. Van Gilder counsels darning as the only effective way to span the distance created by a hole. Darning strengthens the knitted or woven cloth, keeps the hole from getting larger and restores a garment's warmth and protection.

Patchwork quilting resembles darning for what it brings together, though Van Gilder does not list patchwork under that subheading in her book. Patchwork artists on the American frontier assembled small bits of otherwise unusable fabric, often those salvaged from worn-out clothes, into something useful. The patchwork created one large sheet from many small scraps. This whole would then be attached to another sheet of cloth, with fleece, rags or whatever a woman could find stuffed between the two layers. Women stretched these layers on a frame and then quilted running stitches back and forth across the fabric to secure the stuffing. At their best, patchwork quilts reflect the elegant juxtaposition of practical frugality and expressive creativity. The pioneer women who developed the craft seldom had access to dry goods stores for the purchase of new cloth. Even when they did, they did not always have money for such indulgences. Creating artful patchworks and quilting then into warm blankets was an entirely justifiable form of self-expression. Women took great pleasure in applying every last scrap of a certain print or colour to their projects. They invented and pieced elaborate patterns with names that reflect the domestic sphere: Log Cabin, Drunkard's Path, Dresden Plate, Windmill, Variable Star.

Fifty or more years of continued economic prosperity in North America have resulted in darning becoming somewhat of a lost art, though the practice of quilting has continued to flourish. Hundreds of patchwork patterns exist. Women belong to quilting groups or make entire artistic careers out of designing and sewing quilts. Today, quilts are usually constructed with new fabric. It is easy to forget that the essence of patchwork quilting, like darning, is that of making do, of creating some sort of usable sense out of garments that were damaged or worn out.

When my husband and I relocated with our children from Vancouver, British Columbia to a small mountain community in southeastern B.C., I spoke to my mother in California one day not long before we moved. As I stood in the kitchen among the packing boxes and chaos, she said to me, *It feels like you are moving even further away.* I reassured her that I would be coming home just as often to visit, that it was not really all that much farther, from airport to airport. Her reply was faint and not very encouraging. *It feels further. It feels like I am losing you.*

As I observed my mother's illness take a firmer hold of her and begin to alter her vivid personality over those years in the mid-'90s, I was drawn at the time without knowing why to both darning and quilting, skills my mother did not have or pass on to me. I felt a compulsion to understand and practise these domestic arts. Their practice is essentially about making the best with what one has. They spoke to me then as they still do – of recompense and healing, of drawing together, of filling a distance.

About the same time that I took up darning and quilting, I began to practise yoga. I was urged to do so by my doctor, after I fell down a long flight of stairs and badly injured my tailbone for the second time in as many years. I attended a Hatha Yoga class once each week. I learned some of the basic traditional poses, practised breathing deeply through the nose and experimented with balancing on one leg, a particular challenge for me then. When I woke in the morning after a class the night before, I felt like a long wet noodle, soaked as I was in a relaxed fatigue unlike any I had ever experienced. Though I did not understand it consciously at the time, I now know that yoga was helping me accept where I was at that moment in my life: injured, even wounded, full of regret and remorse about my mother's future. When I left the yoga class each week, I felt as if something inside of me had been stitched back together. Sometimes, I even felt peaceful. Or filled with hope.

Restoring cloth or knitted wool involves care, patience and technique, all signs of a strong yoga practice. *From Thimble to Gown* shows a diagram of a hole being repaired. The gap is black and the threads of the darn are white. The book refers to these threads as "ravelings." Each line of raveling, according to Ethel Van Gilder, should be placed about a raveling's width apart. A needle pierces the darkness, marking a path for the newest row of clean, white raveling to follow. Van Gilder says that a seamstress should always use a needle in keeping with the size of the raveling. Lining up the ravelings is a tricky step in the process, because in reality, the new lines of wool raveling do not want to stay in nice neat rows as they are pictured in the illustration. The new threads jostle against each other and sometimes tangle. The second set of raveling threads crosses in and out, over and under the first set in perpendicular fashion, just like a basket weave. In this way, darning calls upon the ancient feminine practice of weaving, the art of making warm and protective cloth from individual fibres.

My mother's illness had emphasized the existence of a widening hole, one that had probably been there awhile, one that needed to be darned. I had not until then consciously considered our relationship to be one that required repairing. But, as I began to restore my own physical, mental and emotional health, I also grew more aware of my mother's struggle and how my own struggle related to hers. I began to sense between us a separation that was asking to be joined. As such, I felt a real and inexplicable impulse to mend. To darn together what has been lost and can never be regained with strands woven in first one direction and then another, to strengthen the frayed bits of her life and mine with a warp and a weft. To connect the original knitted complexity of mother-daughter love with a sturdy patch, resurrecting the usefulness and strength of the whole piece.

With Alzheimer's disease, no precise medical diagnosis exists. Nor is there a cure. No blood test, no x-ray will define exactly what is wrong. No treatment can promise healing or mending a mind in which cognitive gaps have begun to show themselves. We all had difficulty acknowledging openly that our mother was affected by the disease. Who wouldn't, when we knew that there was nothing we could do to improve her condition? As we did begin to acknowledge her situation, the sense of helplessness that emerged from our realization formed an indescribably large hole in our lives.

Whether our family chose to accept it or not, our mother was leaving her earthly self behind; she had stepped onto the road toward death. She had no choice, nor did she have much hope, at least of the kind North American culture is used to articulating when it comes to medicine and health. We could do nothing to heal the damage to her mind. No amount of therapy would alter the physical outcome. We had to summon our courage to acknowledge the changes as they happened, to help her compassionately through the illness, to witness the slow reversal of the human development process that dementias manifest. Neurologist Barry Reisberg first identified this reversal and named it *retrogenesis*, back to birth. According to Reisberg, the stages of decline mirror in exact opposition the stages of human development from birth to physical independence. In the process of attending to our mother's long journey back to the beginning, we began a search for a sort of hope that does not resemble the wish for a cure. We began to make do – to form something strong and usable from the scraps that were left.

I'm not sure exactly when the idea of making a quilt for my mother surfaced in my mind but it was during the time that I was wrestling with feelings of helplessness about what was happening to her and searching for some sort of hope about her future. I recall clearly a special visit home to see my mother and father in order to gather fabric together to make a patchwork quilt. I wanted my mother to choose the colours and patterns and I wanted the quilt to be made entirely from new material.

This was, perhaps, my way of resisting the shabby, worn-out realities of the illness as it is viewed in this culture, of restoring some of my hope and aspiration for her to be whole and well again.

I remember driving her to the fabric store, following the same route through suburban streets that she had taken for me so many times in my childhood to help me purchase supplies for a new project. Inside the store, I led her to the quilter's corner, where a sign had beckoned us. *On sale this month for $2.99/yard.* We stood among dozens of thick bolts of new cloth, every colour of the rainbow, many different prints and designs. I swept my hands around, delighted to offer her this abundance. *What do you think, Mom? What colours appeal to you?* My mother looked totally overwhelmed. Her shoulders shrugged and her eyes drifted into a stare. Still a relative stranger to the realities of her condition, I had been eager to give her the choice. In fact, such an open-ended question of someone suffering from memory loss places that person in utter confusion. Fighting back tears as I realized my error, I began to pull down bolts. *Should we look at the blue fabrics? What do you think of this one? Would yellow go with that?*

Slowly, I coaxed from my once decisive and strongly opinionated mother some preferences. Bolts of well-washed cornflower blues, soft greens, butter yellows, small-flowered prints began to pile up on the cutting table. Her choices were not those I would have predicted, given her past preferences. Her hands, worn and wrinkled by years of housework, trembled slightly as they stroked the stiff, unwashed fabrics. *I have always liked green,* she said. *I prefer soft colours. Flower prints, small flower prints, they are my favourite.* Her faded blue eyes peered out from behind her glasses and a glimmer of the old pleasure derived from looking at cloth and contemplating a new project came clear in her face.

Seeing this liveliness gave me hope. I continued to unfold possibilities from the bolts of fabric, attempting to close the distance between us with yard after yard of cotton. Eventually, we settled on a set of patterns and colours. I hauled the neatly folded stacks of cotton home to Canada in my suitcase.

In the nineteenth century, a beginner patchwork artist often practised her technique on the nine-patch: three rows of three square patches that form another perfect square when assembled. The squares could be assembled in a variety of ways to create endless geometric patterns. As a beginner myself, I admired the simplicity and potential of this method and decided to make a series of nine-patch blocks using four-inch squares. I would connect all the blocks with widths of blue fabric that matched the colour of my mother's eyes.

For hours and hours, I slid scissors along the grain line, chopping up all of the fresh new cotton in a way that would have mystified my frugal female pioneer forebears, as well as the many generations of women who believed that quilting was a way to use up scraps, not create them. As I worked, neatly cut, four-inch squares piled up around me: blue roses on pale yellow fields, lilac peonies on sage green grass, tiny sprinkles of blue and green daisy, fresh-churned butter yellow, the soft green of drying alfalfa hay, a few fluffy, cream-coloured squares for accent.

The spring weather that year was firming up early. I remember it surprising me with its arrival. As I sat in a hot pool of sunshine, patching together squares, my garden beds began to come alive from their winter sleep. Tulip bulbs I had planted the previous autumn sent up pointed leaves to announce the coming of the blooms. Buds on shrubs and trees unfurled their wrinkled ends into supple, bright green flags. The soil took on the deep, lush texture of new growth. I turned away from the work of piecing the quilt top now and then to weed my flowerbeds. I planted sweet pea seeds several weeks late and cultivated a trench for raspberry canes I transplanted from a friend's garden. Then, as all danger of frost passed, I planted out some zinnia seedlings, interspersed with the perennials along my south-facing flowerbeds.

The process of bringing the cloth back together into a whole again honoured my mother and her choices in a way I could not have foreseen. The four-hundred-some-odd squares that I cut and reattached represented not even a few years' worth of school lunches made and packed in brown paper bags, let alone all the dinners assembled, birthday cakes baked and frosted, and loads of laundry hung out to dry and then folded neatly into stacks she would place at the foot of our beds. Stitching together butter-yellow squares in a pool of hot sunshine, I felt in a real way the time she had put into piecing together a family and four childhoods. Years of work as a nurturer, honoured with seam upon seam. Years that dwarfed the hours I spent then on the quilt – dwarfed them into moments.

My youngest son ran in frequently from playing outside, to watch me sew three squares into a long rectangle, then three rectangles back into a square, until nine four-inch squares had formed one twelve-inch block. The geometry of patchwork fascinated his young mind and it wasn't long before he was helping me arrange the various four-inch squares into pleasing patterns. After I had sewn enough nine-patch blocks, I took up the blue fabric she and I had chosen for the sashing but soon realized that I would not have enough of it to connect all the nine-patch blocks into a queen-sized quilt.

Committed by now to the design, I rushed out to the fabric store right away to find a suitable replacement. Ordering almost six yards of a close match, I returned home, quickly chopped up all of the new cotton fabric, then stepped to the sewing machine to pin and run seams. As I laid the nine-patch against the cornflower blue strips, I realized that in my haste, I had cut all of the new blue fabric the wrong size. As my hands trembled and my stomach sickened, an old admonition of my mother's rose through my tangled emotions. *Measure twice, cut once.* Cutting, I realized, was as irrevocable as loss.

The anguish I felt was for more than wasted fabric. I can see now that the patchwork quilt I was making reflected my own healing process, those clumsy attempts to piece my life back together into a whole in a design that would honour my own form of womanhood and grieve for my mother at the same time. I returned to the fabric store and purchased six more yards of blue cotton. It was not hard to rationalize the error, the waste and the added expense. How many times had my mother made a meal that I barely touched, or pressed a skirt that one of her daughters decided at the last minute was not in fashion enough to wear? There are so many unrecognized efforts in the domestic sphere, times when our mothers work for us without much reward or direct result. At home again, I measured the new fabric many more times than twice. I cut only after a deliberate pause. That time, it worked.

Several days later, I surveyed the finished patchwork stretched on the frame together with the bottom layer of cotton and the middle layer of batting. The layers were ready to be connected by the quilting. Quilting stitches can enhance the patchwork by following and outlining its shapes, or they can pick up on a theme in the fabric and quilt another symbol into the project. The closer the quilting lines are, the stronger the final product, an important consideration for frontier quilts made from discarded bits of rag or well-worn clothes. Having used entirely new cloth and a sturdy cotton batting that resists bunching, I was able to develop a design of large hearts with curving lines that connected heart point to heart point.

Sometimes, during the long summer of stitching that followed, I would stop quilting and crawl underneath the frame I had balanced on four kitchen chairs. Lying beneath my mother's quilt, I would gaze up at the patchwork of colours. In late afternoon sunshine, the blue, green and yellow fabrics were illumined like muted stained glass through the layers of backing and batting. The colours had softened and blurred, though the vivid beauty of the combined hues had been preserved.

The body, mind and spirit can be so torn by difficulty that a person feels at times like a pile of scraps. Holes can work their way open in a life, widening to the point that repair seems impossible, reconciliation a faded dream. And yet the art of mending has a magic of its own. Piecing, patching, darning – patient handwork honouring the efforts of those who love us, handwork that comes close to explaining the particular dedication that has allowed sacrifices to be made. As the needle and thread weave over and under, over and under, there is a form of atonement, a way of rectifying losses, the healing of a wound. My mother's work in raising a family may have been her own act of recompense, her very personal effort to mend something within.

The needle and thread offer hope in their quiet, time-honoured work. Through the uniting of cloth and darning of holes emerges a sense that a life may be made useful in unpredictable ways.

JEWEL OF PROTECTION

LATE JANUARY. The Ice Queen clutches a bouquet of frozen and most certain blooms. The petals of these blooms are at once soft with the beauty of snow, hard with unforgiving ice and bleached of any potential vibrancy. The winds screech along the surface of the river down the hill from our house. Accumulated drifts heap and sag in the garden, catching the sun when it emerges and casting blue shadows. Ice turns to a form of blackened stone on the streets and along the fringes of the short path from the house to my writing studio. One evening, as I walk up the hill through the falling snow, I watch fine flakes of snow catch rays from a streetlight as they drift down. The snow sparkles like crushed gemstones, bits of diamond dust distributed into the swirling wind. A car chugs up the hill, its passage muffled by puffs of snow. Around me, the world is so very quiet.

For Christmas, I received a silver bracelet from my eldest son. I enjoy wearing it, having not worn bracelets much since I was a child. It gets in the way of my busy hands as I go about household tasks, asking me to slow down and take more care, to feel and appreciate the slippery, cool movement of this elegant object sliding along my wrist. I have a dream about another bracelet, this one thick and tightly fitted, studded elaborately with large and impressive gemstones of various colours. The dream bracelet has none of the thin, delicate beauty of the silver circle given to me by my son. It is a piece of wrist armour, protective and strong. I wake feeling its cool weight on my wrist, thinking about feminine beauty and power.

I decide to string the remaining seed beads from my vest into individual lengths, with the idea of creating a bracelet from all the lengths twisted together. I know that this exercise of stringing the beads is somewhat of a "make-work" project. I could return to the bead shop and purchase the seed beads already strung into shanks and work with those. Yet I would like to see if I can sustain this work with tiny beads for long enough to create something other than the vest, something that will encircle me. Patience for stringing small beads once came easily to me as a child.

My package of beading needles says they are imported from India, an exotic place in my mind where women wear flowing, silken saris embellished with sequins and beads and bits of gold thread. I have never been to India and I have never worn a sari, but I try to imagine – as I pull a slim beading needle from its paper sleeve – which woman's brown fingers placed the needle into the packet, what colour sari she wore to the factory that day, or whether she had outlined a *bindi* on her forehead before she left the house. I try to imagine whether she suffered from physical or spiritual hunger, or from both.

In 1999, when my mother was near the end of the fifth stage of her illness, my father was diagnosed with cancer. My husband and I flew to the Bay Area for a visit and found my father struggling to maintain his spirits as he began rounds of chemotherapy. On the night before we returned home, my husband tried to revive my father by cooking *osso buco*, an Italian specialty he had always loved. All afternoon, the kitchen smelled densely of tomatoes, browned meat, vegetables and herbs as the time-consuming dish bubbled away. My husband stood at the stove as my father had so many times during my childhood, stirring the sauce expressively, following the tune of an opera aria, sipping a cold cocktail with relish. My father lay in his bed. When dinner was ready, he rose and wearily took his place at the head of the table wrapped in his velour bathrobe. My husband served the plate with great fanfare. But after only a few bites and a half-hearted sip of wine, my father put his head in his hands.

We sat for a while in awkward silence. I had lost all taste for my meal. The music moved to the next track, a live recording of Pavarotti in concert with other artists. As the cabaret-style piano chords settled into an unlikely duet rendition of "New York, New York," my father raised his head. When Pavarotti's rich tenor rose to join Liza Minnelli's husky cabaret voice, a light began to gleam in his eyes. He smiled. After a few more bars of music, he rose from the table with a rush of his old energy.

Come on Mary, he said. *Let's dance.*

While my husband and I watched in amazement, my mother and father circled the kitchen floor, the years taken off them in an instant, the suffering of their combined illnesses lifted away. My mother was again the vivid and intelligent woman he met at a sorority dance, my father was the fun-loving, footloose GI veteran who ran with a group of crazy friends and liked to laugh. The frustration and worry as they raised a large family on a limited income evaporated. What was left? Their deep and abiding commitment to each other, an unseen and important shield against the tragic consequences of their circumstances.

My husband had slaved all afternoon in the kitchen. He could not have predicted that his culinary efforts merely set the stage for the real and only nourishment of the evening. Sick and dying, loyal and loving to his wife despite all the changes to her, no doubt utterly discouraged and exhausted, my father had summoned the energy to celebrate the love and companionship that had brought them together. My mother's smile as she danced in his arms made it clear that despite all her failures of memory, she could celebrate too.

It was not the first time in my life that my father had leapt from the table to dance, or sing an aria, or pour more wine for a guest. He had always been a joyful man at the dinner table. This was different. Here was energy from the human heart overwhelming the chemotherapy and the ravages of Alzheimer's. Transported beyond their personal struggle, my parents proved that strength takes many forms. Some strength is soft and vulnerable; many forms of power are unseen. The two of them moved easily and with surprising grace, transforming the moment into one of beauty and certainty. Here was nourishment beyond a celebratory meal, music beyond Liza Minnelli and Luciano Pavarotti, beauty beyond the material world. I watched them, my father in his rumpled velour bathrobe, my mother in her mismatched clothing. They offered an important clue about how to lead a life, more than how to leave it.

Not even three months elapsed between my father's diagnosis and his death. He died of pancreatic cancer, but his death had to have been hastened by profound fatigue and dispiritedness in the face of my mother's worsening illness, an illness that he refused to discuss openly and candidly right to the end. The speed of his decline gave us little if any time to face the reality of his absence and no time to anticipate how his death might affect our mother's care. When he died, she was still living at home with him and was able to follow daily routine with some independence. *He left before it got really bad*, we sometimes still admit to ourselves.

I visited my father's body before the burial. It was the first time I had ever sat with a dead body. He had been earlier wheeled into the visitation room on a platform. Except for his head, his body had been covered in a tasteful drape. When I was ushered into the room, I suppressed an urge to call out *Dad!* in greeting, as if he were still alive. When I took a closer look at his face, I did not recognize him, so changed was his physical presence. I looked more closely to be sure it was actually him, my father. Faintly, I could make out a facial structure I recognized, a nose that I knew. The essence and energy of the man I had loved was no longer there. Signs of his abundant charisma had entirely left his face, so much so that he did not look physically familiar. His body, I realized at that moment, was not his permanent home. A separation had occurred. A part of him had left.

This experience prompted in me questions I am still pondering about the nature of our physical and spiritual existence, about how these two aspects interact with each other, about where a person's energy goes when he dies. Do we consist of anything permanent beyond the physical body? And if there is such a thing as a person's "spirit," how much does that spirit or essence inform who we are physically when we are alive?

Taoist philosophy suggests that each of us is formed by a balance of energies: that of the body (yin) and that of the spirit (yang). Taoists believe that we are not just physical mechanisms, but energetic beings empowered by *chi* – the universal life force energy. The philosophy of Taoism underpins the way the Chinese describe human life in the traditions of Chinese medical practice. Following an ancient form of healing several thousand years old, Chinese medical doctors believe that a person is a physiological being with organs, a circulatory system, muscles and a skeletal structure, but also a mass of unseen energy. When someone dies, Taoists say that the yin and the yang, the body and spirit, separate. The swirling circle, half dark and half light, breaks in two. Death is called *yin yang li jue,* "the irrevocable separation of yin and yang."

In the time following my father's death, I began to realize that his was not the only energetic separation occurring in our family. My mother was also engaged in a journey across the terrain of her heart. In only a handful of months, my father had grown ill and passed away. By contrast, my mother's separation of body and spirit was taking place incrementally, with painfully slow exactitude.

The glass beads that I slide onto the long, steel needle and then run down a length of sturdy black beading thread are compact if ordinary forms of a jewel, tiny versions of the handsome gemstones that studded the bracelet armour I wore in my dream. They are bright and glittery; a joyous reminder of the miracle of sight. Anglo-Saxon literature called the human eye a "head jewel."

The *bindi*, a beauty mark often worn by Indian women, is part jewel, part eye, a bead of vision painted or placed directly on the skin as a reminder of the *bindu*, the centre of spiritual perception located between the eyebrows. Each morning, on her forehead between her eyes and above her nose, a Hindu woman paints a small circle of *kumkum*, sandal paste, clay or cosmetics. She paints it thickly, so that it will be noticed. The *bindi* she paints is a reminder to use and cultivate intuitive vision, to understand life's inner workings, to look into the past as a way of seeing the future. The spot is, on a mystical level, the sixth cakra, where highly refined perception, intuition, or the sixth sense, resides. This is the spiritual eye that perceives what the physical eye cannot see. Its shape suggests that we can be circles, complete in ourselves. We can be receptacles for divine energy.

Not long after my father died, we moved my mother into a boarding home. She began having great difficulty seeing. When offered a cookie on a plate, she was unable to find it easily with her hand. She sometimes struggled to find the chair she was lowering her body into. At the same time, she was gradually losing all ability to feed herself or take care of herself in any way. The bright look of recognition she had always flashed when family members arrived began to fade. She was unable to call any of us by name, even my youngest sister, who visited her every week. Then, the caregivers reported that my mother's eyeglasses had been lost. My sister took her again to the doctor, where she was checked and fitted with another pair of glasses. These glasses my mother constantly tried to remove. The caregivers were apologetic, but eventually her glasses were put away into a drawer.

While she was no longer interested in visual details, she seemed keenly perceptive about the emotional texture of the family, so much so that we sometimes called her "the vibes watcher." When someone laughed at a joke, she was the first to follow with her own marvelous laugh, one that rolled forward like carillon bells, a laugh that remained unchanged from earlier in her life. She loved our visits, delighted in our hugs and asked us bluntly to stay longer when we got up to go. *Now where do you have to go?* she would ask with childlike affection when a visit had come to an end. As she lost the ability to perceive and understand the physical world, it seemed that her children were becoming hearts that she enjoyed rather than minds that she recognized. We were those who loved her rather than those who accomplished and lived in the material world.

I began to have experiences with her that felt increasingly spiritual. I use this word cautiously and in particular because the significant feeling of those moments was contained in a vessel that no glasses or other instruments of vision could help me focus on, name or understand. I could not see or name what was affecting me so profoundly. "Sight" in our culture usually implies physical vision. We spend lots of time in front of screens, looking at magazines, watching cars fling past us through windshields. We like a "change of scenery." We delight in printed or computerized media with multiple charts, graphs, colours, photos. We put much attention into how each other looks and we judge others largely on that basis. What we see in each other, how we relate to each other, focuses largely on the physical. But "sight" has other connotations beyond the physical that my mother's illness was bringing into focus.

Long ago, the ancient Celtic religion involved the painting of a new moon on the forehead of a young woman gifted with intuitive or psychic powers. Christendom appears to have been the cultural shift that ended the practice. No Christian religion today acknowledges the third eye or how it should be managed. No Christian woman I know paints a *bindi* or any other mark on her forehead each morning before leaving the house, as a reminder to cultivate, protect and honour the seat of intuitive perception. When I was a child, on Ash Wednesday, a priest smudged my forehead with a finger dipped in ash. This was a reminder of the ashes I would become, as well as of the sufferings that Christ underwent before he was crucified. Sometimes, the priest's finger landed right between my brows, on the location of the third eye. *Ashes to ashes, dust to dust.* I remember feeling marked as I left the church with my smudged forehead. With hindsight, I know that the mark was not one rewarding the power of intuition.

In recent years, *bindis* have emerged as fashion symbols. Women paint *bindis* in many colours that coordinate with their clothing. Some *bindis* are made of small jewels that can be stuck to the forehead with a special adhesive. They come in the shape of intricate insects, butterflies, or as a single colourful gemstone. Some more elaborate *bindis* reserved for ceremonial occasions look like a map of the mind, with curving lines of jewel that trace a line above the eyebrow or ascend along a part in the hair. By placing a beauty mark on her forehead at the location of the *bindu*, the Hindu woman affirms not only her visible femininity but also her unseen, intuitive perceptions of a life beyond this world. She oils and combs her dark hair to smooth perfection. She dresses in a sari. If she is married, a traditional Hindu woman paints the *bindi* in red. If she is unmarried, she may paint the circle in black, in part to ward off negative *drishti*. *Drishti* is a gaze without seeing. The negative *drishti*, a sort of "evil eye," might interfere with the purity of a woman's intuitive perception. This negative influence must be protected against, especially in an unmarried woman. The *bindi* can be a symbol of that protection, much as armoured bracelets originally protected the forearm of a man going into battle.

I used to watch my mother apply her lipstick while we waited for my father in the car before leaving for church. She would tilt the rear-view mirror in her direction so that she could see her image in it, or pull a small compact mirror from her purse and hold it close to her face. She would draw the colour on thickly, allow her lips to meet and then roll them back and forth on each other to spread the pigment until the curve of her smile was perfectly, darkly outlined by the vermilion surface of her lips. She looked vivid and beautiful. After that, she would take a tissue from her purse and slide it between her lips, just as one slides a letter into a slot. She would roll her lips on the tissue, wiping off onto the white a measure of the scarlet colour. I found "kissed" tissue sometimes in the wastebasket in the bathroom after my mother had dressed to go out, her perfume lingering in the air. This was cast-off beauty, a remnant of the colour she had chosen to remove from the gaze of the world.

Whenever a woman paints herself, she calls attention to her beauty, especially when the colours are dark or noticeable. I see teenage girls who experiment with wearing make-up in a way I never did. In their search for a feminine identity that will suit them, they try heavy eyeliner, colourful shadow on their eyelids, mascara and glossy lipstick. They are learning what it feels like to be desired, to possess beauty. They are also taking their first steps along the invisible line that separates a good girl from a bad one. In Western culture, heavy make-up is strongly associated with a woman who wants to sell herself, wants to show off what she has, or wants to invite something potentially negative or unacceptable into her life. The line between virgin and whore is a fine one. In social terms, the impact of crossing it can be profound. *Good girls don't wear too much make-up,* my mother used to say. Her comments were both judgemental and protective in nature. She wanted me to take care, to find my way through life unharmed.

Protection involves what a woman does not put on, as well as what she does. This can be confusing. Good girls choose not to flaunt their feminine power, like Bizet's Carmen, or outline it too darkly, like the singer Madonna. They trade their freedom for good girl status. Or, they hold back a full admission of who they are – as an act of preservation.

The ancient teachings of India describe an unseen current of energy that empowers all physical and spiritual experience as *kundalini.* In yoga, energy is seen to flow along a psychic pathway from the base of the spine to the crown of the head, passing through and along seven gateways called *cakras.* Each cakra is associated with a certain quality of energy, with one of the senses and with a specific place on the physical body. On traditional illustrated plates that depict the cakras are images of gods and goddesses associated with that particular energy. Some of them sport third eyes of perception, depicted as a human eye set on its side between their brows. Some of the divinities have multiple heads, each with a third eye. The third eye, or *bindu,* is strongly associated with the Ajna Cakra, the sixth level of energy near the top of the spiral, located between the brows, where women place the *bindi.* The human sense associated with this level of consciousness is the sixth one, intuition. The energy of this cakra represents an essence which some say most empowers beauty.

I spent two weeks in California with my mother immediately following my father's death. During this visit with her, I observed how much her energy was shifting from obvious cognitive skills that can be measured, such as language, mathematics or the ability to tie one's shoes, to less obvious intuitive abilities. One day, I sat with her at the kitchen counter. She sipped a cup of coffee while I worked on a quilting project, a crib quilt for a friend who was expecting her second child. After a while, she broke the silence.

It was awful. I couldn't do anything about it.

I knew that she was referring to the last few days of my father's life, to the agony she must have suffered as she listened helplessly to his moans of pain when he fell getting up to go to the bathroom in the middle of the night, broke his arms and was too weak to get up. She had struggled to dress and waited for my sister to arrive, but she had no ability at that point to act to help him. How much she must have wanted to dial a phone to get help. How much she must have wanted to be able to pick him up, or even to know how to place a warm blanket over him. The hours before my sister arrived early on that Sunday morning to check on my parents must have been very long and troubled ones for my mother.

I know, Mom.

It was awful. He suffered so much. I couldn't do anything.

It's okay, Mom. It's okay.

I placed my hand over hers and squeezed it gently. I picked up my needle to sew some more, reflecting on just how much my mother's heart continued to function despite her inability to care for herself and lead an intellectual life. After several more minutes of silence, she spoke again.

Your father had something in him that he couldn't get out.

My mother's words signaled that she had left the more immediate sufferings of my father and turned to ones that had a longer history. He wrote poetry furtively whenever he could, though he struggled to achieve any recognition outside the family for his abilities. We all possess and treasure the verses he wrote in honour of our birthday, or a visit home, or a marriage. Coming across a box of his childhood mementos in the days immediately following his death, I read letters he had written home to his father while on a ship in the South Pacific during World War II. One letter included a poem. I remember scanning the lines with amazement, realizing that at eighteen, he had possessed a real and graceful poet's voice, a creative voice beginning to speak. In the body of the letter, he asked his father what he thought of it, with a plaintive and almost apologetic air. *It's not all that good, what I've written, but I was moved to write it after that beautiful night on the beach during my leave, and I wanted to share it with you.* The language and images in the poem belied my father's lifelong, apologetic impression of his own gifts.

While my father was disciplined in his professional life and he loved the children he worked with as a school principal, outside of his workday he was more inclined to be a dreamer than a doer. He was haunted throughout his life by having lost his mother at the age of sixteen, and by memories of fire, smoke and death on a ship bombed during the war. My mother was, by contrast, a woman in control of her emotions night and day, focused on her many tasks. It appeared during my childhood that my mother had little sympathy or compassion for my father's conflicted creative self and troubled past. But her few words in the quiet, sunlit kitchen signaled that I had been wrong. She spoke again.

Something was in there. In him. I wished he could get it out. But he couldn't. It made him so unhappy.

Her next few words danced luminously on the sunbeams travelling through the window. They were addressed directly to me.

You are like that too.

I had never discussed with my mother my struggle to achieve a productive creative life, a struggle that had increased in intensity in the year prior to my father's death. I had never spoken about my long inability to establish a clear voice as a writer, to be able to express confidently my view of the world. A high achiever as a child and teenager during my time in the family home, I certainly could not be viewed as a failure. Yet, I had failed, I was realizing at that time. I had ignored my own intuitive voice. As an adult in my late thirties I was still largely incapable of recognizing that my life and my choices were entirely my own to make, that I was the one who could make a difference in my future.

In her book-length poem *The Leaf and the Cloud*, Mary Oliver writes with eloquence and perception of the relationship between parent and child. The voice of the poem describes the parents briefly, only hinting at their impact. The poem speaks of a father of "frustrated dreams" and a mother who "did not always love her life." Then, the words rise with sudden passion. *But I will not give them the kiss of complicity. I will not give them the responsibility for my life.* I have lived most of my adult life a long distance from my mother, my private difficulties largely out of view or conversation. The geographic distance was another expression of the emotional distance I had always felt between us. In those few words – *you are like that too* – she articulated with profound wisdom the task I faced, the task my father himself had faced, the task Mary Oliver describes with clarity and eloquence. Hidden beneath my mother's simple words, out of sight or hearing in this ordinary world, was a call for me to move beyond complicity and toward responsibility.

A shaft of recompense, forgiveness and understanding streamed into the kitchen, riding on the early spring California sunbeams coming through the window. My mother had given me permission to move on. Should I have the courage to do so, she was urging me to begin a life I had never allowed myself to have. Her heart was speaking directly to mine, encouraging me to free myself from past sufferings and embrace my own autonomous challenges, as well as my own possibilities.

Every Tuesday morning, all through the short, cold days of winter, I attend a yoga class led by a teacher named Mary Jo. There are many "styles" of yoga taught in North America. Mary Jo teaches a modified version of a traditional Hindu practice called Ashtanga Yoga, a system dating back thousands of years. Ashtanga means "eight limbs" and refers to the various physical, mental and spiritual practices that inform and support the self-realization process outlined in the Yoga Sutras of Patanjali.

The first two limbs are *yama* and *niyama*, ethical practices related to treatment of the self and others in the world. The third of the eight limbs of practice is *asana*, or the physical poses. It is the asana that have captured so much attention in North America over the past decade, but these poses form only a portion of the entire practice of yoga. Two goals of the asana are to coordinate breath and movement to still the mind and to bring about sweat to detoxify the body. Mary Jo calls sweat a form of prayer. Today before we begin, she explains about *tapas*, a traditional form of purification that results from the creation of "internal heat" in the body through the practice. This heat burns away impurities and makes the body fit.

We begin with a series of Sun Salutations to warm up and follow with the standing postures. As she inspires us to move through the many poses, my mind resists the effort and energy required to persist. I am forty years old, nearly a decade older than most of the women in the class. I look over to Mary Jo. In her forties too, she is fit, strong and flexible. Her presence reminds me that no one is ever too old to meet new challenges, whether those be physical, spiritual, or both.

To facilitate the *tapas*, Mary Jo has turned the heat up high. When I first entered the room, its warmth was a welcome relief from the cold winds of winter. As we move more and more vigorously, the heat grows oppressive. The sweat drips off my forehead onto my mat and my legs tremble with fatigue. More than once, I consider quitting. Several times, the room tips sideways. Once, I drop into Child's Pose to rest. As my breath heaves and my head spins, my mind develops a comforting image, one of rolling up my mat and leaving all the effort behind. I hear Mary Jo's voice. *We are mining the gold*, she says, as she strides past me on firmly muscled legs. *Yoga is alchemy for the spirit*. I rise up and carry on. The class moves through the final standing postures and as instructed, we begin seated postures on the floor, where we practise the Sitting Forward Bend and versions of Half Lotus that open the hips and pelvis.

In the final phase of the hour-and-a-half class, Mary Jo leads us through a series of "cooling" poses that slow our heart rates, including backbends. I am physically exhausted, but I press on to experience the benefits of these final postures. Lying on my back with my feet flat on the ground, I reach back, place my hands behind my shoulders and lift my torso away from the floor. My shoulders arch, my chest opens and my spine extends beyond my mind's prediction. The front of my body flies open. Physiologically, backbends open the lungs wide to more oxygen, stretch the muscles in the upper torso and shoulders and make the spine more limber. But yoga is not just a physical experience. Expanding the chest in a backbend also helps to open the heart.

Walking home after the class, I find myself longing for a bead of perception to take me beyond the sight of the material world. I know that the physical poses are not the extent of the experience of yoga, for me or for anyone else. My practice of the asanas takes me beyond my body to an unseen aspect of human experience, one that I can feel but cannot grasp. I feel this unseen aspect most powerfully in the hour or so after a class. Walking through the small woodland of mixed forest as I near home, I look up to watch a lone raven caterwaul through the canopy of ponderosa pine and fir. The branches dance and moan with feathery freedom as they respond to the unseen force of the wind.

At home, I wash away all the sweat and stand before the mirror, trying different shades of lipstick, some darker than others. I feel like I am fourteen years old again, or younger. I do not rub the lipstick off right away, even though memory urges me to wipe away the most vivid colour, as my mother once did. I stare at the image of myself in the mirror, struggling to overcome the idea that my lips are too noticeable when I paint them. Lipstick resembles the *bindi* in some ways: it is vivid, and one paints it on. Does a woman wearing a *bindi* feel protected enough to express her beauty without fear gripping her heart? Does the *bindi* shield a woman so that she can expose her truest self to the world?

When my infant sons first noticed their hands, they passed them across their face inadvertently, stopped them, wiggled and turned them. In this way, they began to make sense of these appendages as their own. They were someone, actually someone in the world, with a body that could be controlled, with sight that could perceive the physical realities of being. For my mother, the inability to understand how her hand could grasp the cookie or how her body would find the chair was not just one of lost physical sight. It reflected a concurrent abandonment of her personality, a reversal of the capacity to know one's self as an ego, a being separate from others. She was losing the ability to distinguish her physical autonomy. She was ceasing to recognize the hand. But something more was happening in exchange, something in that portion of the mind beyond the brain, that place of perception that cannot necessarily be registered by medical science.

Alzheimer's disease is characterized by what are known as plaques and tangles, microscopic injuries to the tissue of the brain. Do these plaques and tangles affect all levels of perception? How would we know? In a culture dominated by the Cartesian framework that the intellect is capable of perceiving all that exists, we would have great difficulty finding a neurologist who might agree to the presence of a third eye, since it cannot be located on an MRI or even in an autopsy. Medical science has, in fact, determined that my mother's dying process is a long progression of losses without any gains. The culture we live in, one that so often focuses on the material at the expense of the metaphysical, one that defines biological life much more on a quantitative basis than a qualitative one, has fallen smartly into line. This illness is all about loss and nothing else. Very few people outside of my family would consider time spent with my mother to be in any way a positive, gainful experience. They are not lining up at the door to see her, her old friends, her extended family, members of the community. I can understand the reluctance.

How do I explain the benefit of what I have encountered? A form of beauty and grace that does not take visual or even verbal form. I sense it strongly in my mother's presence. Being with her on the path of her illness has me questioning yet again. About the value of Western medical science above all other methods for coping with and understanding the mystery of Alzheimer's disease. About our insistent, narrow definitions of human competence. Even about our desperate search for a cure.

My mother, who has removed her glasses in more ways than one, offers up the possibility of an unconventional sight beyond what my eyes register. She challenges me to look beyond the seen toward the unseen. I am not very good at this, but I am trying. I wonder if her mind is compelled to be busy elsewhere, on the fringes of another life beyond this world. It is entirely conceivable that being able to see the feathery branches on a fir tree, or to recognize the familiar face of an old friend is not the only perception available to us. What are the fir branches, besides fluttering green needles of light offering their vibrant energy to the world? What is a person, besides a face, hair and pair of eyes animated by the inner light of being? Where else can the mind exist, outside of the small, limited focus of this material world?

After I have wiped off the lipstick, I sit with a cup of tea, tracing the carefully outlined mystical circle of the *bindu* and the perplexing, blue-faced gods and goddesses in my illustrated copy of *Kundalini Yoga for the West* by Swami Sivananda Radha. Over the years, my experience of yoga has opened me more and more to the possibility of a spiritual life through these teachings, though they still feel foreign to me. I wish that the culture I spring from could provide me with its own more familiar example of a bead of intuition, a jewel of protection. I would wear this heart-bead more comfortably than a Hindu *bindi*. I can't bear the thought of the stares I would get in the grocery store if I walked the aisles with a red circle painted between my brows. I search the idea of a *bindu* in my mind again and again, looking for a circular clue beyond how dark the lipstick is, for an understanding of why some of the vivid beauty informing our spirits must be rubbed away.

TRAVELLING BETWEEN WORLDS

ONE TUESDAY MORNING in early February, I float out the door of the yoga studio after class. I am stunned by physical exhaustion and relaxation, but also by something else that I have momentarily achieved: a purity of mind known to yogis as *purusa*. In *The Heart of Yoga*, D.K.V. Desikachar defines *purusa* as "something deep within us that is really able to see and recognize the true nature of all things." My encounter with this feeling slows my steps. The sun emerges from behind a winter wall of clouds. It has, since late December, been following a rising arc in the sky. At this moment, I can see clearly how much light has returned – its glare sparkles against ice, moistening it to water in a few places on the sidewalk. Despite the cold, I sense a hint of spring travelling across the air.

I wander down the back alley behind the yoga studio and turn the corner into a small jewellery store, where glass cases are filled with silver necklaces, earrings and bracelets. I greet the owner of the shop, explain that I am "just looking" and begin to cast my eyes over the rich array of polished gemstones and gleaming designs. I stop in my tracks before a striking marcasite necklace that fills a case with its abundant sparkle. Meant to circle the neck quite tightly, the necklace is wide and fan-shaped, a sort of metallic collar.

Marcasite is a cut and polished form of iron pyrite set in sterling silver. Pyrite sometimes takes on the warm glow of gold, hence its common name, fool's gold. The lustrous pyrite and the shiny silver combine in marcasite's traditional setting to create a sparkle that has the depth and richness of many small diamonds. The affordable, steely sparkle was used abundantly as an imitation diamond in art deco jewellery produced during the 1920s and '30s. Marcasite is also known as Thai diamond. I learn from the jeweler and shop owner that, true to that name, this collar comes from Thailand, where craftspeople still enjoy working with pyrite. The geometric, glittering rows interpret the art deco style in a contemporary South Asian style. I cannot take my eyes off it. A few pairs of marcasite earrings sit beside it, but the necklace commands my attention.

Jewellery and precious metals are common symbols of power and wealth that have been used for centuries by monarchs and other political or cultural leaders to command respect and attention. This particular necklace feels as if it is meant for a queen, a female leader like Cleopatra to whom men bow with honour and respect. Eventually, I move on past the necklace, though my desire for it lingers. I leave the jewellery store and stand for a few moments in the February sunshine outside, wiping away tears that have risen in my eyes in response to beauty. A yoga teacher once told me that the neck is the link between the heart and the mind. Necklaces encircle the connecting point, adorning the passage between how the mind organizes reality and how the heart accepts it.

I draw my woolen scarf more firmly around my own neck, a neck completely bare of any glittering jewels. I begin the walk home, feeling a quest for beauty, honour and adornment emerge from a corner of my own true nature. What woman doesn't want to be treated like a queen, or dress like one? But there is more to the marcasite necklace than that. The glittering collar reminds me that material life means nothing unless it marks a firmly established connection between the heart and the mind. The individual shards of marcasite only become beautiful once they are linked into an exquisite pattern, just as a human life only develops meaning when the heart connects with what the mind perceives, forming something resonant and worthwhile.

An object of beauty can honour a woman, or it can lure her. Hades beguiled Persephone with beauty. As a maiden, she was enticed to the underworld by a field of hundreds of the sweet-scented white flowers that he had set to blooming on a hillside. When she reached out with both hands to take some of them in her arms, the Earth opened and she was drawn down, where she succumbed to Hades and became his wife. Persephone left behind a place Homer calls "Mycone," the moon country of virginal dreams. Her mother, Demeter, eventually rose up and took action to salvage the situation, but the beguiling forces of Hades were still too strong to overcome entirely. Persephone could not resist the six sparkling seeds he offered to her. And you know the rest of the story.

Nothing in the surviving classical text suggests that Persephone had any real and willing interest in returning to the Underworld each year. Typically, her original union with Hades is portrayed as a rape and her annual separation from her mother as entirely forced and unhappy. I have begun to wonder, though, if a piece of the story has simply faded from collective memory, whether or not, in fact, she rather enjoyed her reunion with Hades, found him attractive, experienced her time in the dark Underworld as nourishing and worthwhile. She was, after all, Queen of the Underworld. Forced or willing, Persephone's annual journey down required Demeter to forge a different sort of connection with her daughter during that time. Persephone was a traveler – between dormant and living worlds, between the subservient role of daughter and the commanding role of queen. She was a seed that descends into darkness before sprouting up with life again. The rhythms of separation and reunion are embedded in the myth of Persephone and form the foundation for what classical scholars call the Eleusinian mysteries, the procreative powers of renewal.

Beads, like Persephone, travel between worlds. They are capable of moving across vast distances. They make perfect objects of trade, being compact, durable and universally valued. Small carnelian globes from north of Bombay end up deep in China. Jade beads fashioned in Asia find their way to the driest of plateau deserts in North America. Ocean shell penetrates the obscure jungles of the Congo. Indigenous cultures of North and South America moved goods of value and permanence across vast distances by canoe or on foot long before European culture came. Carrying beads as trade items, explorers mapping the Earth several hundred years ago transported them all over. The fur traders arriving on the North American continent from Europe were greeted by indigenous people who also valued beads. A bead could never roll very far on its own. It could, however, be enclosed in a drawstring sack and carried many miles or leagues over mountain passes, across deserts and lakes. Such a bag of beads could be tied to a belt or stowed on a floating vessel. For millennia, beads have spanned distance, enhancing connections between cultures.

So many of us are like the beads, travelers between worlds. Families trade proximity to each other for many things – inviting landscapes, more prosperous cities and career opportunities – as if we were so many beads tucked into a pouch. Our hearts are portable. Or so we think. We often end up far from our biological and emotional source, far from our home landscapes, separated by vast expanses of mind or sky that must somehow be spanned when illness or tragedy strikes. We string the orbs of grief one by one, across the great, unending space that spreads between us. With Alzheimer's disease, the need to span physical distance can be compounded. Separations can be cognitive and emotional as well. Families must often negotiate care and concern from a geographic distance as they struggle to connect even when people live side by side.

The emotional distance I experienced in the first stage of my mother's illness was excruciating because it seemed like a conscious choice on her part. Early on, before we knew what was wrong, it was easy to mistake her growing mental disease as aloofness, or a snub, a purposeful withdrawal. Her refusal to take an interest in a new grandchild, her lack of enthusiasm for social gatherings, her increasing tendency to forget birthdays, these did not seem at first like symptoms of a disease or clear signs of her growing confusion. They seemed like an unpleasant mood, or the heightening of a natural tendency to maintain emotional distance. Denial surfaces and thrives when someone in a family begins to lose mind and memory, when someone begins to be removed slowly and deliberately by death. Yet denial is itself a distancing act.

In *The Forgetting*, David Shenk records and shares the experiences of several individuals suffering from dementia who, in the early stages of the illness, knew what was happening to them. They understood the losses of cognition that were occurring and held conscious awareness that something was wrong. Shenk's record is a revelatory glimpse at the early, internal suffering of victims of memory-loss diseases. They know. My mother's distancing was in part a retreat from confusion, but also a human instinct to want to hide a problem, to disguise a difficulty that might cause disruption or disappointment in her family.

My first and strongest response to the emotional and cognitive distance that the illness inspired was to address the separation geographically. I would drive three hours south across the U.S. border, take a plane a few hours farther south, often passing through two airports on the way, then a shuttle or public transit through traffic to the family home. This process took an entire day. With a young family of my own to care for, my visits to my mother could never be very long. After just a day or two with her, I reversed the whole process and travelled north again to Canada. With each trip over the next few years, with each small act of recompense, pieces of the mother as I had always known her in my memory began to fall away. Gradually, I saw more clearly who she no longer was, and then, most astonishing, I saw the person she had never been able to be.

In an effort to reconnect with and span the distance to a mother of conviction, vivid personality, intense energy, sometimes harsh self-discipline and judgement, I found a different woman, one whom Alzheimer's disease had made more passive, receptive, malleable and soft. Pieces of her memory loosened, crumbling away from the woman she had always been to me. During and after these regular, brief visits, I began to encounter a past that had never happened, a mother who expressed a side of herself that she may never have revealed previously, even to herself. This, in a way I cannot explain, also allowed me a clearer picture of the person I had never allowed myself to be. I realized gradually that there were many beads still in my pouch, beads that could be strung and arranged into a necklace that was uniquely mine. Memory does more than recapture events as they have happened. Memory also stirs and exposes the lost opportunities embedded in forgotten time.

❦

By learning to perforate and string first bone and shell, then precious minerals and finally glass, human culture long ago devised a simple method for wearing beads around the neck. Beads made of all manner of materials became a more noticeable strand when linked together and placed over the chest and heart. Cultures and individuals could adorn themselves with great beauty and individuality, devising expressive patterns of colour and texture. Joan Erikson describes a large number of turquoise and shell beads sifted from the soil near skeletons buried close to Elden, Pueblo in Arizona. When these beads were strung together, they formed a strand several feet in length. Turquoise, the Pueblo Indians believed, stole its colour from the sky. The turquoise and shell sifted from the Pueblo soil linked the Earth and the ocean with the sky, the world above with the world below. A simple strand of bright blue beads, linking mythical time with the hours and days of this world.

My regular visits to my mother eventually became marked by the possibility that she might not know it was me, Eileen, travelling to see her. It happens eventually to everyone who witnesses the effects of a dementia in a loved one. Each of us, all loved ones are forgotten, even when we are fully, physically present. I asked myself, *If a mother does not recognize her daughter by name or face, does it matter that the daughter has come?*

I also realized that my mother did not remember much of anything about my childhood, her motherhood years, or even, beyond a few very scattered details and a half-dozen important people, anything about her own childhood. *If memories cannot be shared, do they cease to exist?* One by one, conventional avenues for making connections with her had been closing off. Visiting her was on its way to becoming an essence of human experience resting outside memory and time, one that called for the heart to assert its presence more strongly in my life. This involved more faith than I thought I had.

The mind's "doing" approach to closing the distance – making quilts, travelling to see her, planting things in the garden for her, bathing her, dressing her – this approach could not go on forever. Connecting with her as I had was, until this time, based on our original relationship as mother and daughter. At some point, sustaining a relationship with someone suffering from Alzheimer's-dementia always begins to seem pointless in the normal context of human interactions, even in the context of the powerful bond between a mother and a daughter. Disappointment chokes out the desire to continue connecting in such a one-sided way. The visits become too painful for many loved ones and sometimes, they cease altogether. If I wanted our relationship to continue in a meaningful way, I needed to make room in my heart. The connection between mother and daughter needed to change. It needed to become more universal, to step outside of the constraints of time and memory.

I planned a visit to my mother on her sixty-ninth birthday the year following my father's death. My younger sister had moved back into the family home to be closer to my mother's board and care facility, and had begun the long process of cleaning and sorting the house in case it needed to be sold. None of us wanted to sell the only piece of the family that remained intact, but we needed to be ready for the possibility. Sitting at the kitchen counter eating my breakfast the morning after I arrived, I looked out the window and saw the pomegranate tree my mother had planted beside the patio. The tree was loaded with globes of the red-husked fruit. Several pomegranates had fallen to the ground, the fruit of Persephone fallen to the Earth, the fruit of remembrance and separation, the fruit of grief and desire. I took a sip from my coffee, watching the tree shiver in the cold, rainy wind. Some of the tough-skinned globes on the branches had split open, exposing rows of polished, deep-red seeds. A squirrel hopped along the fence toward one of them, intent on gathering the jeweled fruit.

Until that moment, I had forgotten all about the pomegranate tree, though of course it made sense that this Mediterranean tree of ancient and mythic proportions could survive in California's mild climate. I tried to remember when my mother had planted it. It may have been soon after I left home as a young woman, during that time when I was reading Proust with intellectual affectation and feeling that life with any meaning at all must revolve entirely around French history, culture and art. No doubt about the time the tree was planted I intended then to be totally unlike my mother, even though I had, according to many people, a strong physical resemblance to her.

I heard my voice speak out loud in the quiet kitchen. *The tree must be almost twenty years old.* Internally, I counted the rapid progression of years, the row upon row of ruby-red seeds that had brought me here, to this point. Somehow, time had ripened me from a young maiden enthralled by French culture to a mother in early middle age, a woman with school-aged children who took long-weekend trips to sit in silence with her dying mother, a woman negotiating her way through a dense forest of losses.

The pomegranate tree's thick trunk rose straight up, a proud spine supporting a web of arms, their bark grey as November skies. The leaves, small and numerous, glowed with the bright, exotic yellow of saffron. I stood up, opened the sliding door and walked through the damp wind and rain to stand beneath the shivering tree. As I reached high in the branches for pieces that were whole, I thought about Demeter's grief, a maternal grief so consuming that for a while, she completely abandoned her work as goddess of the Earth's fertility. It was a grief I could relate to, both as a mother and a daughter. There are differences, of course. In my own personal chapter of the myth, the mother is the one whom the Fates call away. The daughter is the one whose fertility is compromised. And yet, the desire to transform loss into renewal remains the same. Having chosen two of the best fruits, one for each of my sons at home in Canada, I stepped back into the house. I sat for a while at the kitchen counter, rubbing the dull, thick rind, a uniform husk that protects the complex, symmetrical rows of seed hidden inside.

When I arrived at the board and care facility to visit my mother later that day, I sat with her in a well of silence. I wanted to talk about the pomegranate tree, to ask her if she remembered how her friend Florence Klinger used to take a bag full of the fruit from the tree each year to make jelly. Florence was a spry little white-haired woman who always brought a few small jars of clear, garnet jelly back to my mother in exchange for the gift of the fruit. I said nothing of Florence and the jelly, knowing that the recollection would be one-sided. Instead, I reached forward to grasp my mother's hand. She allowed it to rest in mine for a few moments. Then, with no explanation, she withdrew it. I watched her place it on her pant leg. She smoothed the fabric several times. The withdrawal was a small death, a retreat at once unexplained and unbearable. I did not reach to grasp her hand again.

I had travelled one long day of car and plane and airport delays in late autumn weather to come to this place beside her, to help her celebrate a birthday that may have meant very little to her at all. I had followed a trail of pomegranate seeds into the dark woods of separation, where they ended abruptly. There was no sign of where to turn next. I could not find any bearings. She had not been able to greet me by name. She had removed her hand from mine, proving to me in this brief gesture that the space between us must somehow be closed by other means.

When I flew back into Spokane in early evening on the return leg of the trip, I stepped into a dark and snowing world. Frozen flakes swirled toward the ground like torn wisps of Persephone's white wedding veil. The drive north from the airport through arid, ponderosa pine woodland and then into the densely forested, mysterious mountains where I live was an ordeal that again tested the logic of my dedication. As I crawled along through the accumulating slush and snow, I began to wonder if the weather was a punishment for my clumsy attempt to close the distances between my mother and me in such a physical way. I should have known that simply taking trips to see her would not accomplish what the heart most needed.

Driving in a heavy snowstorm, I always feel the world grow smaller and smaller as the flakes enlarge and the drifts pile higher. The horizon shrinks to the confines of the car and a few feet of visibility that precede and follow the glowing globe of headlights. The claustrophobic weather conditions outside the car that night felt not unlike my own mind, as I replayed over and over within its small mental space the challenges that my love for my mother now faced. I crawled along the formless road through what was usually my favourite part of the drive, along the natural twists and turns of the Pend Oreille River. But that night, in the dark and snow, I felt an eerie lack of familiarity and a quiet distaste for the landscape's gloom. I could not see the river I was following. I could not perceive the terrain I loved: its soft riverbanks and splendid trees, the fields of bracken tarnished by autumn frost, an occasional barn filled with hay, spires of coppery larch tree flickering to a point as their flames lit the hillsides. To guide me as I drove deeper into the darkness, I had only a berm of snow between one set of fuzzed tire tracks and another, a faint sign of the road, illuminated by the weak and struggling beam of my headlights.

When I crossed the border into Canada at Nelway, Washington, I began the last stretch of the drive through the narrow mountain valleys. The snow continued to fall steadily, piling up on the roadsides, dimming further the glare of headlights, making vision more difficult. With eyes stinging and shoulders cramping, I pulled off the road at the entrance of an unlit rural driveway. The snow kissed my face as I stepped out. I strode a few steps toward a bank of evergreens at the edge of a field, taking in a few great lungs full of the cold air and tried to loosen my shoulders as I scuffed through the drifts. Energized by the cold air, I began to stride farther.

As if the Earth had opened before me, I felt overcome by the depths of the darkness, the white pain of the torn sky overhead. I felt suddenly lost in the winter-dark world – unveiled, vulnerable and afraid. With thoughts of a stalking cougar rising in my mind, I turned and rushed through the deep snow back to the vehicle, locked the doors and started the engine. As I swerved onto the main road toward home, the two pomegranates rolled across the back seat, seeking a purchase that is impossible for any sphere.

That night, I acknowledged finally, without any competing texture of denial, the lonely, unmarked way of grief as I followed a snowbound winter road marked without so much as a sprinkling of garnet seeds to guide a heart's way. I knew that my mother's illness would be an increasingly solitary experience for my siblings and me, one that would either strengthen our bonds to each other or undermine them, one that might offer the four of us no other companion but faith.

⚓

A few months after this visit, I began to dream about my mother both while awake and when asleep. In the dreams, my mother sometimes appeared as one who suffers profoundly. She was either physically ill or in great mental anguish. Though she looked like my aging mother in these dreams, she acted much like a terrified, helpless child. I would wake feeling the full onslaught of the distress and loss that define her way of dying, my way of grieving and the struggle of our culture to accept the reality of Alzheimer's disease and other related dementias. In the unhampered space and time inspired by sleep, my heart seemed to link to hers in defiance of the pillow my head rested upon, a point so far from her physical location. The dreams transported me out of the realm of conscious, individualized memory into a collective place, a place marked by a sprinkling of glass seeds, where I can be reminded that my mother's suffering is my own.

In other dreams, my mother appeared youthful, aspiring and beautiful. She was dressed in her wedding dress – a frothy skirt of tulle studded with hundreds of tiny sequins. She twirled freely in the sunshine, as if she had not a care in the world. Or in another, she ran lightly after butterflies in a field of alfalfa planted by her father, trying to capture some for a high school biology experiment. In this glittering, fresh-promised world through which she danced, she defied the dusty, perspiration-soaked realities of her own mother and father, who struggled to make a living on an arid desert during the depression and war years, who persisted through drought and times of plenty. I wrote these sparkling and hopeful visions down as they came to me, attempting to preserve and validate them as memories, even though I had no way of knowing if they ever happened.

Both day and night dreams of my mother began to occur vividly only once she slipped cognitively too far from my grasp to make a conventional relationship with her at all possible. This convinces me more than anything that memory is the mother of imagination. Memory forges a relationship with the past that can at times appear to be like a future taking shape. The task is not only to remember. It is to witness the memories, and then to practise a heart's discernment. To measure which memories to let go of, which ones to string together into a new order, and which ones to hold just as they are, beads rolling freely in the palm of a hand, beads attached to each other by an almost invisible fibre of meaning.

I think of the lush but shortening days of September in these mountains, when I sometimes encounter a spider's web in my garden that appears to float in midair. So far from the web are its fixed points of attachment: the branch of a rosebush or fruit tree, the stem of a perennial flower. What an experience for that spider to weave its lacy snare in such a way. To take a leap into the air's windy uncertainty, plunging across the distance from one anchor in search of the other one not yet seen or felt, perhaps only imagined. I used to point out these floating webs to my two sons when I discovered them, hoping that they would perceive the extraordinary defiance of security and abundance of faith that the webs demonstrate to me. They sway strongly in the breeze and yet are attached by a fibre of such slim iridescence that it can be perceived by the mind only with great effort. When my sons rushed off to play again, I would stand in the golden light, overtaken for a brief moment by feelings of aspiration. I watched my boys go, wishing not for their material or social success, but for their ability to span distances more effectively than I have done, to spin webs anchoring them firmly to the unseen.

I recently met with a Native elder, a spry woman of the Sinixt (Arrow Lakes) tribe named Eva Orr. I was researching and writing a book on the landscape and history of the Arrow Lakes people in Canada and I hoped for her endorsement of the project, her permission to write about her people's tragic loss of their legal status, their very right to live and exist in their home landscape. After we spoke for about an hour, I got up to leave, asking her if she would mind speaking to me again sometime. She looked up at me. *I would like that,* she said, taking my hands into hers and standing up. Then a sparkle of warmth and certainty, like a piece of marcasite, rose in her eyes. She let go of my hands, lifted a necklace from around her neck and placed it around mine. I had been given my answer.

Formed by linking common bead to common bead, the necklace offered to me by Eva Orr speaks eloquently of the need to connect race to race, person to person, heart to heart. None of the beads are gemstones of great value. The necklace is made up of ordinary shell discs, a few tubular lengths of polished bone and several aquamarine blue plastic faceted spheres interspersed with shiny, royal blue plastic discs, strung in patterned groups of ten. They form a quite ordinary array that is far from the commanding glitter and presence of the queenly marcasite collar. Humble but no less powerful. Eva's impulse drew together our disparate worlds. Beads strung to relate hearts across cultures, across continents and across the mysterious and often unspoken distances that have formed between us.

The making of connections can be, as Demeter and

Persephone discovered, an act of renewal, a creative and sustaining force that holds within its own Eleusinian grasp the potential for life lived abundantly, pomegranates stuffed to bursting with polished seeds, a garnet sweetness and complexity to feed the human spirit.

THE ROSARY

FEBRUARY IN THIS STEEP MOUNTAIN VALLEY can test
the endurance of even the most optimistic and cheerful soul.
The days are often grey as well as cold. The inland temperate
rainforest seems to call the clouds toward it, deepening the darkness. And yet, almost imperceptibly, the light in February grows
brighter and brighter with each passing day. On sunny days, it
sparkles and dances across the snow, casting blue shadows in the
hollow of a drift, or the trail forged by a dog or deer. Inspired by
the outdoor brilliance, I think about wearing the sparkly copper
vest. I've worn the skirt several times, but I have not had the
courage to put on the vest. I grow listless in the approach of my
forty-first birthday. My birthday comes and goes – with the vest
still hanging in the closet.

On a visit home to my mother last year, I came across two
rosaries in the flannel-lined shelf at the top of her cedar chest in
the back bedroom of the family home. They both appeared to be
very old. One is a series of tubular mother-of-pearl beads linked

by a chain of finely worked, age-darkened metal. The other is similar, except that the beads are oval and black. My mother could not tell me during that visit which women in her family used these rosaries, though she must have remembered at one time.

I was the Catholic daughter of a daughter of a daughter, all three generations raised in the teachings of one of the oldest of Christian faiths. At the age of eight, I received my First Communion – dressed traditionally in a white voile dress, my hair capped with a lace veil. Just before puberty, I passed through the rite of my First Confession. On Fridays before significant feast days or holidays like Easter or Christmas, I participated in the Sacrament of Confession with my mother and siblings. I stood in line before a dark, carved wood confessional cabinet. When it was my turn to step inside, I whispered nervously to a priest hidden on the other side of a sliding screen, describing how I had failed to be good.

I cannot recall what my sins were thirty years ago, but I can easily reconstruct the sensation of fear that I felt when I made my way to the stuffy confessional closet. Inside, the air smelled of must and varnish. After I confessed, the priest would give me "penance" for my sins: a series of well-practised prayers that I was to recite as I kneeled before the altar of the church. Five Our Fathers, Six Hail Marys. Two dozen Our Fathers. Ten Hail Marys. The penance varied, depending on the priest, the sin and the time of year. On the drive home with my mother and siblings, I felt a relief that I mistook for having been purified.

In the Middle Ages of Western culture, male leaders of the Catholic Church frowned on women who wore jewellery. Rather than forbid the wearing of beads or gemstones, however, the priests transformed their use from one of adornment to one of faith. Beads were strung into prayer counters, commonly known as rosaries. While the earliest Christian church appears to have rejected prayer counters as guides for what Jesus called "vain repetitions" in the Gospel of Matthew, by the Middle Ages, their use was common and even encouraged.

Beads of glass and gemstone adapted easily to a new life as devotional spheres in the medieval Christian world. The word "bead" actually descends through the language from the Old English word *gebed*, which means "prayer." In Middle English, the word became *beden*. It was closely related to the German word for prayer, *beten*. Beaded prayer counters were heavily used by pious individuals called beadswomen or beadsmen. These people were hired to pray for the soul of a benefactor. Individuals who could afford more than one patronized several beadsmen or beadswomen to pray voluminously for them. The rosary beads helped them achieve salvation. After death, the beads would stay behind on the miserable Earth, having served their purpose stringing a path to heaven.

Rosaries are mnemonics, objects to assist memory in the recitation of a specific order of prayers. I used to watch old women in the church fingering their rosaries during the confession service on Friday afternoons, the dark, glittery beads on the rosary mingling with the black lace of their prayer veil, or *mantilla*. The women kneeled forward toward the altar, moving their lips around the air, sliding gnarled fingers from one bead to the other as they made their way through the cycle. Each bead was a reminder of where they were at that moment – in a timeless space between the past and future of their invocations. It held them in the present. The prayers they uttered would have been learned in Latin, as my mother and her mother learned them prior to Vatican II: the *Paternoster*, the *Ave Maria* and the *Gloria*. I learned them in English in the aftermath of the Papal Reform, and though I once knew the prayers by heart, I am embarrassed to admit that I now struggle to get the words right in all three.

Christians picked up the use of the rosary from pagans, a word derived from *paganus*, those who dwell at home. This term originally referred not to non-believers, but to the Romans who stayed home tending gardens while the *miles*, or soldiers, travelled Europe in conquest. The word rosary also derives from Latin. *Rosarium* is the ancient word for rose garden. Rosaries in Roman antiquity and early Christian times were often made from rose petals strung together fresh, or from petals that had been dried, crushed and formed into small beads. Similarly, Arabic poets called their rosaries *wardija*, or rose garden. They viewed white and red roses as feminine emblems. The Muslims use strings of 33 or 99 beads, with one leader bead. These strings guide them as they repeat the 99 names of Allah found in the Koran, plus the one essential name. Muslim prayer counters are commonly made of wood or date pits.

Those who practise yoga or meditate often use a string of 108 beads called a *mala* to track the number of repetitions of a *mantra*, or incantation to the Divine. The number of beads is said to relate to the number of names for the Divine Mother, though this number may have other, unseen significance. The repeated mantras can be as simple as one single syllable or as complex as many Sanskrit syllables piled upon each other to form devotional phrases thousands of years old. Repetition of mantras is said to activate the spiritual force, as well as clear the mind and teach it to focus.

Mala is a Sanskrit word meaning "garland" or "chaplet." The *japamala* was the Rosary of the Mantras. In *Kundalini Yoga for the West*, a garland of beautiful forest flowers called a *vanamala* is draped around one of the male gods, Visnu, he who preserves. Many of the gods and goddesses depicted in the illustrations of the kundalini cakras wear malas. The malas used by Hindus are traditionally made from the dried seeds of the Rudraksa plant.

These small, reddish-brown seeds are said to represent the eyes of Siva, the male aspect of the Divine. They have a rough texture that gradually grows smooth as the fingers pass over and over them, following the cycle of prayer. Hindu malas can also be made of crystals or other beads. Buddhist malas can be made from black lacquered beads, sandalwood, small stones or inlaid animal bone.

As with the rosary dedicated to the Virgin Mary and framed by the Our Father and Glory to God, inherent in the design of the mala is the awareness of both a divine nurturing female force and a creative male force. The interplay between masculine and feminine energy in the universe – Siva and Sakti, yin and yang, God the Father and Mary the Mother of God – can, in the vision of many religions and philosophies, create a sacred balance that brings harmony to the Earth.

My mother's daily routines have become a sort of prayer cycle, a string of events that, if broken, results in increased mental chaos and psychic desperation. The caregivers in the home where she lives understand the significance of routine and repetition. In a cycle that appears dull and tedious to those of us caught up in the dictates of the past or the excitement of the future, life for my mother and the other four residents of her small board and care home revolves around the steady acts of the present: waking, bathing, dressing, dozing, eating and sleeping. They live here and now. They watch Martha Stewart with riveted interest, these women who will never hold a kitchen knife in their hands again.

The board and care residence where my mother lives has a shabby but spotless central living area. There, a ring of white-haired women often sit in an arc around the room: one leaning forward on the couch, her hands on a walker; two others bright and upright in chairs, watching Martha Stewart blanch leeks on the television; one more very small and birdlike, wrapped in a crocheted blanket, sleeping. Beside this little bird in her nest on the couch I often find my still-dignified mother, her white head of wavy hair framed by her permanently shrugged shoulders, her hands folded neatly in her lap.

I have learned to approach my mother physically as well as verbally. I will sit down beside her, place my arm around her in a hug and greet her. *Hi, Mom, it's your daughter, Eileen. I have come all the way from Canada, just to see you.* Sometimes, she responds with a bright look and a smile. Sometimes, she looks confused. Usually, she answers my hug with a willing, gentle expression of her frail form. *Oh, how nice*, she says, as if I had come to deliver some milk.

Does prayer require language? It begins as a conscious act, a memorized utterance repeated over and over with the mind's help, or as an invocation formed uniquely to reflect the distress or gratitude that has prompted it. *Dear God, or Hail Mary, or Allah.* At some point, though, prayer can enter the unconscious realm, to take the mind beyond the suffering or the limitations of this world. This happens through chanting, meditation on a certain Zen *koan,* or through the multiple repetition of prayer cycles with a rosary or mala as guide. Some say prayer must take place entirely in this expanded present in order to be truly effective. That is why prayer often has a focal point, to hold the devoted one in the moment. Prayer transports someone outside of the reasoning mind, that aspect of ourselves from which language emerges as a conscious utterance. The language builds a bridge, and a devoted person uses it to enter a sacred inner place and leave behind the aspect of mind that loves to measure, compare and judge, that feeds on what we have versus what we don't have.

I have often asked myself if making a long journey to sit beside a woman whom I cannot be certain knows I am there might be considered a sort of prayer. I have come to see my visits to my mother as their own form of invocation. They are my clumsy, unpractised, unconventionally religious attempts to bear witness to her suffering, to observe and honour her shrinking mind, to accept her expanding spirit and to hope for her release.

A few years ago, while my father was still alive, I took my mother to mass one day. She was very pleased to be there. I noticed that she had difficulty with the recited prayers and responses of the mass, but this did not affect her pleasure. Recently, the language my mother utters has moved even further from consciousness. And yet she continues to verbalize, far more than is "normal" for the later stages in the illness. Some days she is more talkative than others. She repeats phrases in a nursery cadence and sometimes makes up words to rhyme sounds. *Purd to the bird......take him home to the toil to the tile......mexie rexie......'cause a necky recky, he said "no"......Nancy came in and she said "no, we can't go home"...... on the top on the tie......the boys the boys the boys......we don't want pink because they look awfully toffly......*

The verbiage spills from her: names, common nouns and two- or three-word sentences, made-up words and unintelligible phrases or repetitions. In this shattered verbal stream, semantics has been overwhelmed by the plaques and tangles of her mind. She talks, but doesn't make much sense. A student of language all my life, I often listen in fascination, scribbling the phrases down on the back of a discarded envelope that I have dug up from the bottom of my purse. I am also horrified. My mother's once supreme intelligence clearly expresses the effects of the neurological chaos she endures. Some names are recognizable, others are not. There are also moments when it seems that she is offering a bead of truth to whomever listens, a cogent phrase that rises up among all the others. As if it was aimed, like an arrow, directly at my heart. *I love you.* Or *Thank you.* Or *God bless you.* And then the veil of incomprehensibility falls again. *No, we can't go home......the boys and the boys and the boys......no, no, noooo, no......he said "no, we can't come home".......* I want desperately to know if the words indicate that she is, deep inside, sorting something emotional out behind this stream of language. I want to find out if she knows where home is, and how to get there. But I doubt I ever will.

Once, I encountered my mother in a quiet but distressed mood. As I sat down beside her on a couch and put my arm around her, she looked sideways at me with suspicion and anger and said, *No, I don't want that like that. Just leave me alone.* She sputtered more angry words. I made every effort not to recoil, but instead reached toward her again, murmuring in a soft voice. She collapsed into my arm with an anguished sob. *My father my father,* she said, as her frail shoulders shook and her head bowed toward her chest. She uttered more words I was not able to discern. It was clear that her suffering on this Earth was not yet complete. I rocked her back and forth in the crook of my arm, murmuring what words of comfort could rise to my lips. I was astonished by the weight of her anguish and even more astonished to realize that the path toward a heartfelt life does not lead to a place without suffering, just to a place of compassion.

I do not pray on a daily basis, though my Catholic upbringing would suggest that such a discipline could help my mother. She is unable to use a rosary now. If I did, I would pray for my mother's release from earthly existence through an act of grace, a supernatural gift of God that leads to salvation. This gift of grace would be beyond nature, intended for the next world, the life hereafter. Catholic theology specifies two types of grace: sanctifying grace (of the sort Adam and Eve had before the Fall and that any individual has before committing a mortal sin) and actual grace, favour from God. Actual grace can come through the use of a rosary. The concept of grace has deeper cultural origins in classical mythology, where it is defined as beauty in action. The three Graces were emanations of Aphrodite, goddess of love. Hospitable, attractive, generous and kind, these cousins of the Muses expressed beauty freely. In Sanskrit, grace is called *karuna*. It is a combination of beauty, kindness, mother-love, tenderness, sensual delight, compassion and care.

I have not attended mass in at least twenty years, other than a few times in my father's memory, just after he died. I have not raised my sons in the Catholic faith. In my own modern, cynical way, I grew to see the prayers following confession as some sort of cheap exchange for a woman having crossed the line, a way of her being able to buy back some of the goodness lost or a way to sustain herself passively through difficult times. My highly trained, postmodern intellect wondered how it was that prayers could buy any form of salvation or get anyone off the hook. This was, I perceived, a deal offered to a girl by a man positioned behind a pious screen. The beads on the rosary seemed to be made of guilt, not devotion.

Now, softened by middle age, my mother's suffering and my own, I understand how the rosary could stand for devotion, how a mala could guide worship. I understand that prayer is more than an act of barter. Prayer expresses faith and focuses intention. Prayer develops into music when words are recited over and over. It is a graceful act, one that can call a form of beauty into a life. I have, many times during my mother's illness, wished that I possessed my mother or grandmother's simple loyalty to their Catholic faith, that source of strength outside of themselves. Their God might well have given me some sort of support. He might have provided me with a well-lit way through the dark forests of self-doubt and anguish. He might have helped me to pray for an end to my mother's tortured parting from this world.

As important as her faith was to my mother, it was perhaps a form of divine grace that she ended up in a board and care home staffed almost entirely by Philippine Catholics, whose faith and gentle compassion permeate their daily tasks. The routines of my mother and the other residents are framed by caregivers who speak almost no English but are fluent in the language of loving-kindness. There are always at least two of them present, often three. They chatter in Filipino with soft, musical voices, move with quiet grace and exhibit no frustration whatsoever with the physical and mental limitations of their elderly charges. They take excellent care of the residents, and they do so with compassionate hearts. I hear them in the kitchen sometimes, chattering away with ease and enthusiasm in their native language.

One of them has a shrine to the Virgin Mary in her room: a statue of the Virgin, some plastic flowers and a rosary strewn across a cotton cloth. When a resident dies, the caregivers always light candles and perform a nine-day cycle of prayers known as a *novena*. Novenas are specific Catholic devotions performed for specific reasons; in this case, to comfort the spirit of the person who has passed away.

These are the real heroes of Alzheimer's disease, my younger sister is inclined to say. I have also come to think of them as a modern form of beadsmen and beadswomen, those whom we have hired to care for our mother, those whose faithful behaviour moves beyond the limitations of verbal language. They give care in a way that defies words, with such gentleness, humour and respect for humanity that it provides some passage away from earthly suffering, helping to ease the difficulties experienced by the ring of white-haired women.

☙

Early one morning, I wake drenched in sweat, breathless and full of fear. It takes me a few minutes to recognize where I am, and where my mind has taken me.

I dreamt that I was in the back seat of an old sedan, travelling with my mother and grandmother. We were headed across a field on the ranch where my mother grew up, to a white clapboard house where my grandmother and grandfather lived as newlyweds. I have a photo of my grandmother holding my newborn mother on the porch of this small, white house. My mother's tiny face squinted into the fierce California light, my grandmother's bare arms were smooth and strong. As we drove across the field toward the house, the road beneath us transformed from the blond, withered grass of central California's summer savannah into a lush green landscape. This landscape passed beneath the rolling car like sidewalk paintings depicting a tropical paradise: tangled broadleaf trees, heavily scented flowers bursting with bloom, rolling hills of lush grass. I watched out the side window, amazed by the colour, vibrancy and growth. As the three of us entered the front yard of the little house, the green growth disappeared. Butchered cattle lay in heaps on withered, grey-brown grass. Dust and blood pooled around them.

Was it my grandmother or my mother driving the car? I cannot remember. The dream ended abruptly, when we arrived in the front yard of the little house.

My mother's mother was born Grace Drew Skinner, just after the turn of the twentieth century. Her father was a banker in Alameda, California, near San Francisco. My grandmother lost her mother when she was eight years old. No one seemed to know for certain how my great-grandmother died, though I had heard my mother say more than once that it may have been the result of mental illness, perhaps even a suicide. There always seemed to be a cloak of secrecy around my great-grandmother's death, whatever its cause. So young when her mother died, my grandmother may never have been told directly by her father what happened. Or she may have known and wished to keep the suicide secret, to avoid the shame about such a death, shame that would have been common in that era, especially for a Catholic. Committing suicide is, in the eyes of the Church, a mortal sin.

I have begun to wonder what exactly happened to my great-grandmother. I suspect her loss is relevant in my own struggle to accept my feminine role, as one of the "memories passed through the mother-line" that Carol Lee Flinders considers part of the cultural collective of being a woman. Recently, I asked my mother if she knew for certain how her mother's mother had died. She looked momentarily confused, then shook her head. This was a memory lost to time, a memory that could not be researched through conventional means.

After my great-grandmother's death, my grandmother was cared for by a nanny named Louisa, a woman of whom she was very fond. My great-grandfather remarried four years later. This marriage apparently set my grandmother and her younger sister apart within their family as a new set of children was born. In 1922, my grandmother received a diploma in modern language from the College of Holy Names, a post-secondary Catholic school in the San Francisco Bay Area near her father's home. A few years after that, she boarded a train and travelled south three hundred miles to teach school in the small rural community of Pozo, California. I try to imagine how it must have felt for her to arrive at a small, dusty train station in San Luis Obispo and be met there by a school trustee, who loaded her baggage into his model T and began the hot, four-hour-long drive into the rolling hills until they reached the new settlement of Pozo with a one-room school in a stucco building perched high on a hill overlooking a few stores and buildings marking the main street. On the one hand, she must have felt great freedom; on the other, fear.

Soon after her arrival to teach in this rural school, my grandmother met my grandfather, a tall, handsome man with dark wavy hair who was also a fine hunter. His father was a successful merchant, his mother descended from German immigrant pioneers. My grandmother eloped with my strong, handsome grandfather in 1927 – without her father's permission. She drove hundreds of miles east across central California's desert into Tonopah, Nevada, where they could be married legally and quickly.

The hope and promise of their early days together fell victim to time and circumstance. My refined and educated grandmother was not the best equipped to be a rancher's wife. The depression and drought of the late 1920s and '30s made achieving prosperity a true struggle. With the closest Catholic church an hour's drive away, I suspect my grandmother missed often the opportunity to attend mass. As the years passed, the respective faiths of my grandfather and grandmother were tested in so many ways: by nature, by their private grief, by struggle to succeed. My grandfather built the ranch into several thousand acres, but not without great emotional and physical sacrifice, extremely hard work and a singular focus on survival.

Down down down over there, my mother has taken to saying lately. *We need to get water down down down over there.* She points her finger, indicating a direction that only her mind can understand. She repeats it several times. *Down over there. Water down down down over there.* Her worried mumblings about drought and her directives about where to find it all suggest that she lives in and experiences her past as if it is happening right now. These words hint at the struggle her parents had to succeed in ranching through the depression and war years. My grandmother must have felt the need to rely on her prayers more often than not. She must have wished that she could transform the arid California savannah into a lush, tropical paradise.

The ancient texts of Indian culture, the Vedas, describe a great river that once flowed down out of the Himalayas into the Thar Desert, to bring life and abundance to people living along its banks. The people called this river Saraswati, after one of the three most prominent goddesses in Hindu culture. Saraswati is the goddess of truth, knowledge and speech. She is often depicted wearing a white sari and a mala made of pearls. Some say Saraswati means "she who has lakes or pools," or "one who flows." *Sara* in Sanskrit also means one who gives the essence and *swa* means of the self. The goddess Saraswati's gift to the people was the abundant flow of her own essence, water that purified, inspired and nourished, water that symbolized the flow of words.

The ancient Saraswati River sustained the flourishing Vedic culture, where people believed that the path to a soul's liberation was marked by the acquisition of knowledge. The Vedic period of art, music and literature in ancient India strongly resembles ancient Greece for its celebration of learning. The abundant and reliable flow of the Saraswati River was the voice of a landscape. It kept the people fed and supported the development of high culture, among which was the first written communication in India. To this day, Hindus view the goddess Saraswati as one who guides self-expression.

Today, the once lush river basin is a dry memory in the desert. Around two thousand years ago, seismic activity blocked the source waters of the river in the Himalayas, causing them to divert another direction. What was a flourishing, green world of art and life quickly became an expanse of gravel and dust. And yet, geologists have recently discovered that the Saraswati River may still be flowing through that dusty basin – far below the ancient riverbed. Drilling in the desert has unearthed surprising and abundant sources of water. A river can be dead and diverted on the surface and yet maintain its liquid path far below.

The rosary and its accompanying prayers must have been a rare form of water flowing deep in my grandmother's inner life, a constant source of strength and vitality. Even if I choose not to follow my mother's and her mother's specific path of faith, I must somehow retrieve within myself the innate ability to worship. I must find my own source of strength, necessary for the times when the water seems to dry up completely, when the blood of loss eclipses lush, green growth. I have witnessed a mother and grandmother who knew how to forbear, how to pray and how to worship within dogma. I need to learn to clasp my own hands in prayer, to flex the worship muscle. The beads on the old rosaries are smoothed and darkened by hand oil and countless use, reflecting a tireless, timeless focus on a divine power that offered comfort, instruction and strength. They symbolize faith that has met the test. They remind me that in my strenuous but sometimes contradictory rejection of Catholic dogma, I have nearly ceased to value worship.

Stripped almost entirely of memory, my mother exists for the most part in the present. There she sits. Do I have the courage to follow her into the moment, to sit close beside her in the silence? She is not dead and she is not without value, despite cultural marginalizing or rejection of elders who journey through an illness that is at once tragic and outside of our control. My mother's real presence on the Earth despite her mental and physical infirmity continues to guide me toward a centre I did not know I have, one that can only be achieved through a relinquishing act, an abandonment of the heaviness of the past and future, where our attachment to material gratification of many kinds weigh us down, among them our intelligence, our youthfulness, our histories and our accomplishments. If we are not careful, my mother has taught me, our memory will tie the weight of our beings more firmly to their sufferings, rather than set them free. If we are not careful, we will find ourselves defined from the outside-in, rather than the inside-out.

Accepting her as valuable despite her infirmity has required me to let go of how she has been in the past, of how she might have been in the future. It has required a leap of faith. Watching her mind lose its hold on personality and language has provoked a profound sense of loss. This loss was experienced by my father before his death, and it has woven itself into each of her children's lives as we cope with the final stages of her illness. But loss cannot strip away everything. There are some aspects to humanity, some aspects of being that persist despite loss or even death. These are moments of prayer, sources of constancy. They emerge to define us as valid and loved no matter how much we have suffered, no matter what twisted form our physical and mental selves take on the surface of this Earth.

Is it possible that Alzheimer's disease has risen as an illness of our time because of something we need to learn? Relinquish the mind. Let go of the hollow husk of material being. Embrace a power beyond human accomplishment. Accept mortality. See then what happens. When I cease to reason my mother's presence, or try to understand or even grieve for it, I experience my mother's being nonjudgementally, in its immediacy, however it comes. If I can accept her without subtracting her condition from its past losses, without measuring her condition against those of others who seem to be aging in an "ideal" way, I may have entered a state of true devotion to her life and her being. There, in a swirl of collective memory, sits a bead of great beauty and virtue, a sparkling centre of meaning, a mother to our imaginations and our potential.

When the feminine moon passes in front of the masculine sun in a total eclipse, the overlapping of the two planetary bodies blocks bright light and plunges the Earth instantly into darkness, no matter the time of day. During this total eclipse, rays of sunlight line up around the outside of the moon's sphere in a chain that resembles a string of beads. Astronomers call this scientific phenomenon a rosary. Might it be possible to reach into the dark swirl of cosmos to grasp this rosary as I pray? This brilliant garland of light reflects the totality of nature when sun and moon – creator and nurturer, masculine and feminine – overlap to worship the divine possibility of a balanced, healthy Earth.

WILDFIRE

WINTER CONTINUES TO CLING to the mountains as February draws to a close. I journey south to see my mother again. I am anxious for spring, a season that takes its time returning to mountainous landscapes, with snow clinging to high peaks and cold, rainy wind swirling in the valleys. The progress of bud and blossom is slow. Complex mountain geographies always produce idiosyncratic, sometimes turbulent weather cycles that turn back on themselves, slowing the progress of spring. By contrast, spring will be well underway in the far more open and temperate climate of California – there will be rolling hills lush with the moist velvet of young grass, cherry trees in the full flush of pink blossom, daffodils poking open faces out of warm garden soil. I anticipate arriving in this splendour. I imagine finding my mother as soft, peaceful and ideal as the season.

When I walk into the board and care home the morning after I arrive, it seems that her physique has shrunk noticeably in just a few months. She has lost weight since my last visit in

December, the knife of time quickly sharpening her features. I search her face, but see little if any light in her eyes. When I sit beside her, she appears to be absorbed in a mumbling conversation with herself. Phrases begin intelligibly, but after a few well-formed words, the sounds she makes diffuse into a primitive recitation. These are utterances, not speech. When I put my arm around her, she barely shifts from her delusion to turn her head. Winter has followed me south. I have found my mother one step closer to the darkness of dormancy and end. This dark energy has not been so strongly evident on previous visits. Or perhaps it was an aspect of her departure that I was not until this visit willing to perceive, ready to accept.

Death is not always a beautiful sight to behold. Of course I always knew that, at least intellectually. Demeter, the great mother and goddess of all abundance, also oversees decay and death. My father's death was a decided dose of the practical to add to my theoretical understanding. Yet Alzheimer's disease has provided a stage for death to display its ugly reality so painstakingly that I have had to render a more and more detailed scene of the effects of loss as I work across the canvas of my mind. In the way that it so gradually undermines the capacity for reason and the function of the physical body, this illness is a portrait of despair. It is unrestrained in its threat to darken the human spirit and distort individual personality, in its anger, its unhappiness and its rudeness. All of these are aspects of the mind that exist, every day, in all of us. They have not been invented by the disease. The disease has unmasked them, laid them bare, exposed them to my eyes.

As I sit with my mother, I know that I am being challenged to come to terms with the darkest aspects of the mind so that I can continue to be present for her during the last phases of her illness. Continue to love her unreservedly, honour her completely and respect her without judgement. I am being shown the unrestrained, instinctual nature of her decaying mind. The mind possesses, like any other capacity, both a dark and a light aspect. This dark and light – the spiritual gifts as well as the raw physical and mental disappointments of her illness – co-exist in my mother as they do in me. The dark and the light may even depend on each other.

Taoist philosophers say that the feminine force of nature is dark, yielding, receptive and related strongly to the Earth. The yang, or masculine, is on the other hand, bright, active, exterior and noisy. It relates strongly to the heavens, to spiritual aspiration. In the Taoist universe, these forces interact constantly to create balance in the natural world. They complement each other and even require each other to sustain energy. The feminine principle, often symbolized in Taoism as the Mysterious Female or the Mother Earth, is at once enigmatic in its darkness and obvious in its earthiness.

English Renaissance humanists also related the Earth to feminine energy. The Earth was, during that period in Western culture, a nurturer of great kindness and generosity who provided for the needs of human beings, a gentle and yet majestic force of the Great Mother, that abundant and nurturing force also known in other cultural periods or traditions as the Divine Mother of sacred yoga texts, Demeter the harvest goddess of ancient Greece, or Our Lady the Virgin Mary in Christianity. Yet, nature in the Renaissance of England also expressed the chaotic and uncontrollable aspect of the feminine, the perversion of nurturing power. Women were either weak human beings who yielded to their uncontrollable wild instincts, or overpowering individuals who accessed and expressed their instincts too freely, sometimes with imposing consequences. In the English Renaissance, the feminine was both revered and feared – for its ability to nurture, and to destroy.

In India, the power of a woman's destructive force displays itself in the Hindu goddess of destruction. Kali, the dark and destructive aspect of the Great Mother, is the cutting edge of truth, she who burns away all illusion and past mistakes. She puts old concepts to the flame and in doing so, she can destroy or overpower what a right and rational mind thinks is best. Often depicted with her tongue hanging out and wearing a necklace of skulls, she ravages anything that is not real and is, in the words of Barbara Walker in *The Woman's Encyclopedia of Myths and Secrets*, "simultaneously womb and tomb," the procreative and nurturing mother as well as the terrible mother, the angry destroyer.

What does it mean to be completely wild, to be governed by the real quality of instinct? Wild places have not been altered from their original, natural state. No culture has controlled, managed or contained their freedom. Earth turning on itself, a sun rising and falling on its arc, animals and plants following the dictates of the seasons. Bears lurking in the woods. Storms blowing up, rivers flooding, avalanches roaring down steep slopes, fire sweeping across hillsides. Destruction as well as creation, always hand in hand. Nature tugs at the dark and mysterious unconscious, that inner aspect that hosts our instinctual origins. The origins of our own wildest and most elemental beginnings as human beings reside in this unconscious place. It is in the dark corners of the mind that the powers of reason falter.

In the mountains, when the softening spring air brings on a beautiful fluff of blossom and rush of green leaf, it also quickly melts the winter snow, turning our valley's slow-moving rivers and creeks into a white riot. The necessary transfer of energy from snow to water, such a life-giving and essential process for the landscape, takes place in a context of chaos and uncertainty as creeks rise toward the top of the banks each spring. Nothing can stop the process of melt once it begins. Nothing and no one can dictate the rate at which the melt takes place: how much snow has fallen the previous winter, whether the weather will speed or slow the process. In this annual, cosmic uncertainty resides a form of chaos and unpredictability that can only be called *wild*. We can only hope that the destructive force of the water will not overwhelm its nurturing capacity.

What I see in my mother is a mirror of the wild instincts I have so often denied in myself and those whom I love. The sounds tumble out of her mouth like one of the wild creeks flowing over its own banks. She seems unable to control herself. How can I reconcile this uncontrollable mother with the one who raised me into adulthood? When my hand passes inadvertently near her face to wave to a resident on the other side of the room, she opens her mouth and thrusts out her tongue – as if to accept food from my hand, even though it was empty.

My younger sister and I bring my mother back from the board and care facility to the family home, where we set her up on a chair in the middle of the kitchen floor, to give her a haircut. Instinctively, she knows something is up even before we begin. She has to be coaxed into the chair like a resistant animal. I feed her pieces of cookie one by one, to keep her sitting as long as possible in the chair. My mother lifts her arm to swipe the hand holding the scissors whenever it approaches her ears. She shakes her head like a resistant child, rising from her chair and saying, *No, no, God damn it, no.*

Flames from Kali's fire lick up around me as I help my sister. I distract my mother with another cookie, holding her firmly for as long as I can so that my sister can take another snip of hair with the scissors.

I have always sought great delight and comfort in the natural world. I have been inclined even to idealize wilderness, to romanticize the "original" state of landscapes prior to European conquest as one of perfection and gentleness. I see in my mother something that cannot be idealized, something that exposes the limitations of my thinking. She is simultaneously a creek rising higher and higher and a fire set by Kali's rage. The illness has engaged her in a process no one can control. And its impact on me may not be so easily controlled, either.

⚓

As a student in France twenty years ago on an art history field trip, I stood one day before portals in a church dating from the Middle Ages. I do not remember the name of the church, or even which city it was in. But I do remember clearly the carved stone narrative of lives condemned to hell's fire or eternal damnation because of their sins, the grotesque agony and suffering of their weighted souls. The sinners' heads were enlarged, their bodies wizened, their faces contorted by fear. Standing in the church, I wanted to turn away from them. I listened to the highly refined, intellectual prattle of my art history professor who had stopped our group in this spot for an impromptu lecture on stone carving: ... *et ici on voit les visages torturés, les yeux énormes les corps maigres... On voit les pécheurs.* The name of this spry, passionate teacher has, all these years later, escaped my memory even though the precision of his words has not. He always peppered his lectures with the verb phrase *on voit. One sees,* he would say in French. *One sees this, and one sees that.* This was his way of reminding us that art was about seeing clearly. *On voit... on voit.*

Standing on the cold stone floor of that church, my mind fraying at the effort of following the rapid, constant stream of French words, I was not able to comprehend all the intellectual nuances of his lecture on the history of religious art and the religious symbols in the carved medieval portal. I had only this simple verb phrase to anchor my understanding. *On voit... on voit.* In the dim light of the old stone church, he had asked us to open our eyes, to perceive with historical understanding how the Middle Ages depicted life beyond the mind – life after death, if you will. Here was an outcome of religious extremes, either of heavenly or hellish proportions. Never anything in between.

I was deeply disturbed by the carvings in the portal, as I was when a few months later I stumbled on an exhibit of surrealism in the museum of modern art in Paris. The work of Magritte, Man Ray, Miro, Ernst and Giacometti expressed again an aspect of humanity that made me shudder: distorted bodies, headless figures, a flatiron studded with steel spikes of torture, a young girl relishing a songbird with her teeth, blood dripping from its feathered corpse down onto her chin. Working as artists in the 1920s and '30s, when Western culture had begun to plunge into the depths of the unconscious through the psychoanalytic research of Freud and Jung, the surrealists attempted to show what they believed to be the "super real" function of the unconscious mind: an almost chaotic free association of all that can happen, all that has happened, in an inner life. They were not, like so many generations of artists before them, driven by an aesthetic will to make things ordered, balanced and beautiful, but instead by an ardent wish to unveil honestly the full, natural spectrum of the human psyche. Here, in the shattered geometrics, abrupt collages and incongruous associations, was the mind in absence of the controlling faculty of reason. Here was the illogical content of thought unleashed from any aesthetic preoccupation with goodness, order and light.

Though I could not understand it at the time, the surrealists were commenting on the origins of hell and suffering, which contrasted sharply with that of the Christian Middle Ages. While both the stone carvings and the canvases depicted aspects of human darkness, the surrealists demonstrated that we contain entirely within our minds the full emotional spectrum of paradise and hell. There is no need for an external destination, they seemed to be saying. The mind can take us there itself.

Young and idealistic, increasingly confident with the developing knowledge of another language and culture, carrying my copy of Proust's nostalgic, sun-drenched memoir under my arm, I wanted art to be exclusively beautiful. I had no interest in suffering. As my immersion in the language and culture stretched into months, I began to dream in French, expressing myself even unconsciously in a language beyond my mother tongue. This was a moment of remarkable happiness and freedom for me. I cut my hair in a stylish way and was filling notebooks with the thoughts of a young woman coming into herself. In the midst of this exploration, I wanted the sweetness of life to be consequential and democratically deserved. I craved idealism, in whose warm light I believed I might bask and flourish toward my full womanhood.

Strolling through churches and galleries, that young idealist could and did strenuously reject both the medieval carvings and surrealist canvases, at least for a time. I turned my back on their horror and incongruity. I cultivated an interest in what I saw as the true beauty: the fruit and flower porcelain wreaths of the Renaissance sculptor Della Robbia, the sunflower fields of Van Gogh, the bright, star-studded paper cuttings of Matisse. An innocent still, I was incapable of perceiving that beauty only receives its weight and significance from the compensatory world of suffering, chaos and death. That love and loss form a sphere of light and dark, a beaker containing a potent elixir heated by Kali's fire. This is an alchemical mixture of idealism and realism, a potion that is both perfect and flawed, bright and dim at the same time.

I was incapable of absorbing then the reality that my mother presents to me now: that sometimes, one is born into one's truest self not from careful cultivation in hothouse splendour, but from struggle in a cold, unforgiving environment – from uncontrolled rage, from ugly truth, from shattered illusions. There, when it seems that emotional survival is impossible given the harshness of the conditions, one encounters the final limit to rational understanding. While I spent twenty industrious years avoiding that encounter, my experience with my mother's illness has finally brought me to a place where I can throw up my hands.

Why? Why must she suffer this way? I have asked myself this question so many times, it has worn a groove in my mind. There is no answer, no rational reason. I have followed the struggle for theories detailed in the media. Theories invented by modern, scientific minds in search of understanding on a physical plane: that the disease results from exposure to aluminum, or from too much of this or too little of that, or from a certain gene that some people carry and others do not. That it can be staved off by regular practice of crossword puzzles, or by drinking less coffee, taking certain vitamins, keeping oneself fit. While pharmaceutical companies search eagerly for some sort of cure or therapy, the origins of the illness continue to elude them, as do any cures. The attempt to explain and understand the illness is an extension of a cultural habit we all practise: that what happens to us is somehow consequential, or that we can choose the way in which we depart from this world. That we can control the outcome, rather than submit with grace to a destiny over which we have little control.

I know that my mother does not deserve this, that she did not choose this. I know, too, that like the surrealist images I once found so distasteful, what has happened is horrible. This is a horror that I must accept. *On voit,* my art history teacher used to say. Twenty years later, my task remains the same. To open my eyes and see. To burn away illusion and accept both the darkness and the light of human experience.

Beauty, the illumined aspect of the grotesque, a possible antidote to all that is distasteful, unkind or uncompromisingly wild. Yet, like the grotesque, like anger, like death, beauty is not something manageable and controllable, something one can separate exclusively from the rest of human experience as a pleasant and pleasing experience. Van Gogh's vibrant sunflower fields sprouted, in the end, from the dark soil of his own confusion.

On the last evening of my stay, I know I should visit my mother one more time before I pack my suitcase for the trip home. Yet I find myself deeply reluctant to go. My hesitance exposes my hypocrisy and my fear. It is possible that I remain afraid of and willing to reject my mother's infirmity. It is possible that my perception of her beauty and worth that has arisen during her illness can be eroded. Was I the last in my family to realize the full spectrum of the tragedy? Standing indecisively in the kitchen, I feel betrayed by my own blindness, my own naiveté, and what I perceive increasingly as the stubborn hold my mind has on illusion.

My younger sister, who visits our mother week after week with tireless devotion, has understandably elected not to go back for a second time in the day to see her. I will be going alone. I try to tell myself that I do not have to go, since I have seen her earlier in the day. But to see her is really the only reason I had come all this way. To see her. *On voit... on voit.* There is no justification for staying away, other than weakness or distaste. So I climb reluctantly into the car and drive to the nearby board and care home. To see my mother. To see her.

It is dinnertime when I arrive. I guide my mother to the table, kneel beside her and begin to feed her. One of the caregivers offers me a chair, but I shake my head. As I feed her, her hand thrusts forward to the plate. She grabs a piece of carrot, then a chunk of potato, and shoves them into her mouth, smearing food across her fingertips and onto her lips. I wipe her hand gently each time. She always insisted that we learn to eat politely, as she had been taught by her mother. She believed that manners were a passport into any world we might wish to explore. Still, when she sits in a chair, she automatically crosses her legs in a ladylike way.

After dinner, I lead her back to the couch where she likes to sit. I sit with her for a while, listening to her diffused mutterings. As the light fades outside, I shift on the sofa cushion, preparing to get up. *I need to go now, Mom,* I say. She does not reply. As I rise up, she rises instinctively to go herself, as if to say, *If you're going, then I'm coming too. No, Mom,* I say, putting gentle pressure on her shoulders to guide her back down to the couch. *You need to stay.* She does not appear to understand. I sit back down, and she follows me into her seat. When she seems to be settled, I hug her for a few minutes and rise again. She, too, begins to get up. This time I am faster, and with a quick kiss on her soft, pale cheek, I head for the door. Leaving, because I must.

It is difficult to greet the ugly face of death, but it is perhaps more difficult still to be able to leave a loved one in its grasp.

When I land the next day at the airport in Spokane, Washington, the afternoon light glitters across late-winter patches of snow that still dust the arid ground. As the February sun drops to my left, I decide to take a longer route home, one that will take me along Lake Roosevelt, a reservoir formed from the dammed

Columbia River. I drive directly north across the plateau to connect with the fertile farmland of the Colville valley and catch up with the Columbia's reservoir. My car rolls through snowy fields not yet ready to wake into spring. I turn onto the highway that follows Lake Roosevelt, a placid stretch that was once a rumbling, uneven and wildly twisting river. Heading north along the shores of the reservoir as afternoon fades into evening, I notice the waxing moon, rising above the mountains in the east. As I turn east in the last leg of my journey home, I follow the lunar bead, hanging like a pendant on the dusky throat of twilight. It has been a difficult visit home, more so than they often are.

THE FLOWER-BRINGER

THE CALENDAR TURNS TO MARCH. Snow softens. Drifts shrink toward mud. The ground reappears and widens until patches of frozen white remain only in shaded corners. Branch buds become noticeable. The air bristles with possibility and the streets run wild with rivulets of melt. I hear new birds chattering. The brave chickadees and solitary ravens who have wintered here are joined now by pine siskins, juncos, crows and flickers. The diamond-bright sun of February has been replaced by a milky light, a thick custard that fills the Earth's bowl above my head.

Near the end of the first week of March, a late cold snap seizes the valley. The extreme grip stops spring in its tracks. Frigid winds blow hard down from the arctic, rattling the bones of the trees, testing the endurance of the Earth. Though I am reluctant, I take a cue from the weather. I retreat once more into a dark cave of thought, thinking about the possibility that winter might never end, that my mother's illness might go on forever.

A dozen finches passing through the neighbourhood hunker down at the bird feeder outside my studio window. The finches cluster at the feeder, nourishing their tiny, lively forms. They appear undeterred by the setback in the weather that has me staring morosely out the window, wishing for warmth. One night, a gardener who helps me prune my fruit trees phones to postpone his visit until the weather eases. I tell him about the flock of brave little finches. *They're called a charm,* he says. *Isn't that lovely? A charm of finches.*

I listen with only half an ear as he suggests dates for later in the month. The next day in my writing studio, I watch the birds more intently through the smooth pane of glass and the austere haze of cold. I notice their feathers, painted with bright brushstrokes of red and yellow. The colours they wear call the Earth toward renewal, when male seeks out female and another cycle of life begins. The finches seem so alive, as if they have a great and sustaining faith. I sense joy. And there is something else. Yes, something else. A charm has arrived.

My older sister has, like me, become a mother. She is attentive to her children's needs, devoted to their well-being, gentle with them in manner and voice. She speaks to them as if they are her friends, as well as her children. She is a wonderful mother. It seems to be an added affront to the loss of my mother that I also live distant from this older sister, that we are each so busy mothering that we often have no time to share our stories with each other, to trade notes and to support each other in our work. She, like me, lives one long day's travel from my mother. She, like me, visits my mother with regularity, when she can. We are seldom in California for these visits at the same time, though we try to send each other reports on how we have found Mom when we return home. We are mother ships passing in the night, two women raising children, two daughters sharing the same maternal loss.

My younger sister, my older sister and I form the points in a feminine triangle that stretches from California, east and inland to the Midwest, then north and back west to British Columbia. The three-pointed, sharp-angled space between us is often a challenge to span. Within this space sits our mother's illness, something that separates us and at the same time holds our three sides together, keeps them from toppling in. The past several years have been challenging for the three sisters. More challenges lie ahead. We are being asked, as much as we possibly can, to communicate clearly with each other, to cooperate in our mother's care, to ease her sufferings, to make the most of the situation.

The triad is an ancient feminine shape. So often in world religion and belief systems, the trinity comes up. Some of the oldest versions of this three-part divinity in human civilization are formed by women, or multiples of three women. In ancient Greece, the archetypal mother manifested three ways: as Hebe, the virgin, Hera, the mother, and Hecate, the wise old woman, encompassing the emotional and physical evolution of a woman's life. The Fates and the Graces each were powerful female trios who, on the one hand, controlled destiny with their spinning, and on the other, presided over the beauty and charm of the natural world. Three Sirens sang their haunting music to Odysseus and other sea voyagers, threatening safe passage home. Three Furies positioned themselves with vengeance, their heads covered with serpents, their claws and teeth bared. In ancient Rome, there was the female team of Luna, the moon, Diana, the Earth, and Proserpine, the Underworld. The three aspects of Devi, the Great Mother in Hindu faith, also formed a triad: Durga, fiercely protective, Kali, the destroyer, and Parvati, "she of the mountains," benevolent, charming and a good wife. Another feminine trinity in Hinduism, known as a *trimurti,* consisted of Lakshmi, wealth; Parvati, charm, and Saraswati, art. Kali had three heads, as did Egypt's primal mother, Mut, and the Celtic goddess Brigit. And then there are the Muses, a tripling of the original triple goddess of ancient Greece, nine women who inspired and informed the development of culture.

With the advent of Christianity in the West, the female trinity of antiquity began to break apart. The first Christian trinities were a mixture of male and female, with God the father, Jesus his son, and Sophia, the highest development of wisdom and spirit in feminine form. Sophia was, in the earliest Christian and Gnostic churches, the mother of the soul, a source of inspiration to inform the power of God. In *The Great Goddess,* scholar Jean Markale details another vestige of the ancient triple goddess in the Gospel of John, where he finds references to three different Marys who stood near the cross the day Jesus died: Mary his mother, Mary of Clopas and Mary of Magdala. In the end, Markale suggests, the number of Marys in attendance was not a coincidence. This triad appearing in the Gospel is, he believes, an echo of the Great Mother in her three aspects, a veiled reference to the ancient cultural worship of a feminine trinity.

As the Christian church spread across Europe, Sophia's dove (originally the bird of Aphrodite, goddess of love) gradually became the primary visual symbol for the Holy Spirit. Direct references to the feminine spirit disappeared. The trinity I encountered in church was that of God, Jesus his son, and the Holy Spirit (earlier called the Holy Ghost), pictured as a dove or simply as a shaft of light. While Mary, the virgin-mother-of-god, was important in her role as the woman who gave birth to

Jesus, she was placed more firmly in the theological background. She embodied the virgin mother portion of the triad, but not the wise woman, the Sophia-of-the-soul. This feminine aspect of high spiritual development and power had disappeared. I grew up making the sign of the cross and reciting the Catholic trinity: *in the name of the father, son and the holy spirit, amen.* I remember learning about "God in three persons." These "persons" (the father, son and the holy spirit) felt entirely male to me. The masculine triad was a remarkable deity, one in which was invested omnipotent strength, compassionate humanity and spiritual power. I made the sign of the cross whenever I entered a church as a symbol of devout belief in a power beyond my own. I wore a small, gold cross on a chain around my neck, bright like the sun.

The weatherman forecasts that the cold snap will continue for a few more days. The finches chew ardently on the black sunflower seeds. I top the feeder up frequently, in a misguided attempt to hold the winged charm in my yard. The truth is that the birds have come and will depart entirely of their own choosing. They are wild, and they have wings.

Even as the icy winds whistle around the house, I comfort myself thinking about spring, about the abundant charm that will soon enough burst forth in my garden in the form of blooming fruit trees, bulbs planted last fall, roses, perennials and wildflowers crowding for space at the fringes. I set out plastic trays for starting seeds and rummage in the back of a cool closet for packets left over from last year. As my mother's illness has embedded itself more deeply in my life, I have placed more importance on coaxing from the Earth a frivolous form of beauty and charm that need not be justified by a fruit that follows. I love to grow flowers.

I grew up in a household of ardent vegetable gardeners. I do plant some produce, tomatoes and carrots and cucumbers, but I strive more than anything to cultivate blooms. As I dampen the soil and scoop it into the seed trays, I think about Thalia, the third of the three Graces. She is sometimes called Flower-bringer, as well as Good Cheer and Charm. While all three of the Graces presided over the beauty and fertility of the natural world, Thalia, in particular, connects to the adorning power of the Earth, to the blooming and flowering of trees, shrubs, vines and other plants. She carried flowers with her all the time. Flowers helped her charm the gods on Mount Olympus.

I sprinkle the small, papery arrows of zinnia seed into several pots and cover them lightly with soil. It is hard to imagine that these inconsequential bits of fibre will sprout into large, lush plants by midsummer, plants that will fill the small bed of soil beside my front door with a host of bright pink, yellow and orange flowers, cushions upon which the butterflies will rest. Dozens of them at a time will suck pollen as the summer matures, their gossamer wings sighing back and forth. Next, I fill my hand with the dark pellets of four o'clocks, also known as the marvel of Peru. Though the mature flowers refuse to open until late afternoon when summer light is less fierce, the hard seeds need the brightest possible light to germinate. I place these little beads directly on the surface of the soil, nestle them in a bit, dampen them with a spray bottle and cover them with clear plastic.

Trapped indoors by a mountain climate that wakes slowly to spring, I beckon Thalia and her sisters, Aglaia and Euphrosyne with my tray of seeds, these beads of the Earth filled with potential to adorn and inspire. Perhaps I will be able to cultivate a form of charm in my garden that has not taken hold naturally in my life. Daughters of Zeus and Eurynome (the latter a nymph whose own father was Ocean), the three Graces are at once liquid and firm in their beauty, fragile and enduring. A relief sculpture from the fifth century BCE depicts them standing side by side. Though their heads have not survived the sculpture's journey across time, the curving bodies and shifted hips remain as a visual hint of the reverence ancient cultures placed in the fertility, beauty and grace found naturally in women. A nineteenth-century marble sculpture of the three Graces by Antonio Canova interprets them in all their exquisite, refined elegance. Canova has carved a scarf that wraps through all three. The women face each other in a modified triangle. They are perfectly poised. Their hard marble flesh looks soft and alive.

While two inspires balance, three provides substance and creates a shape. Two, it is said, accounts for *both*, but three accounts for *all*. Three becomes a community, a shaping of lives. Plato believed that the atoms of matter making up the universe took the form of triangles, that this three-sided geometric figure was the basic building block of the entire material world. In the triad of women weaving its way through time, I feel the stability of three goddesses, three women, three parts to divine energy. I sense in the tri-part virgin–mother–wise woman and in the three sisters who spin or bloom or spew fury an abundance of the *all*. The triple goddess expresses the opportunity for each facet to be part of a whole, expanding spirit. A spirit that is born, flowers into beauty, ripens into fruit, then slowly dies to make way for the seed's future.

And yet how impatient I can be. It is so hard for me to leave the seeds to their own rhythms of readiness once I have covered them with soil or clear plastic. Indoors or out in the garden, I always stalk the places where I have planted seeds, checking sometimes daily with anxiety to see if they have risen above the Earth. I poke at the soil with my pinky finger, searching. Yes, I know this disturbs them and threatens their survival. I know I would be better off to leave them alone, to allow them to spring toward the light in their own good time. The teetering movements of my faith make it difficult to leave them lie, to trust that they will rise up unassisted into the world.

On a visit home to see my mother several years ago, I helped her purchase and plant a rose bush to replace one in her garden that had died. We chose a hybrid tea called the Peace Rose. I had strong memories of this lovely rose from my childhood. It bloomed in a pale golden yellow with blushing pink cheeks. As a child, I sometimes asked her if I could take a rose to my teacher and I always wished it would be the Peace Rose in the right moment of bloom to clip and carry away. My mother would come out with me to the side of the house where her small rose garden was, to choose a rose that was not too far open, then help me wrap it in a bit of wet paper towel, followed by a scrap of aluminum foil to trap the dampness inside. I would hold the rose carefully in my lap on the bus ride to school, trying not to bend the stem or bruise the petals. There were other roses, a dark red one called Abraham Lincoln and a deep pink one whose name now escapes me. It was the Peace Rose that I always loved the best.

That day several years ago when we replanted the Peace Rose, my mother held a garden spade and stood beside me while I dug the hole and filled it with compost. I watched her make a few odd thrusts at some hardpan nowhere near the hole I had started for the rose. It was clear that though she wished to be involved, she no longer had the capability to plant and tend. I said nothing, then turned my attention back to the hole. As I placed the rose into the hole and patted the soil back around it, I felt a wave of pleasure that I thought at the time came from her. I wonder now if it was actually my own. A pleasure that rose like a tendril of hope, reassuring me that memories of a favourite bloom might be somehow preserved if I could replace a plant that had died, perhaps of old age, perhaps of neglect.

My mother saw my garden here in the shadow of high mountains only once. Just after we moved to southeastern British Columbia, she came north with my father to visit in the middle of May. At the time, some of the spring perennials I had planted the previous year in a warm, south-facing place were beginning to bloom. She followed me along the edge of the developing flowerbeds on a sunny day, admiring the irises and peonies. I picked a small armful to arrange in a vase for the dinner table. She came indoors with me and together we stood in the kitchen at the counter. I clipped the stems of the deep red and purple flowers and placed them in water. Her fingers traced delicately along the petals and her eyes grew warm with appreciation. *I love arranging flowers,* she said softly, though really, it was my hands that were doing the work. I had never heard her say such a thing, in such a soft voice.

She went on to tell me about the flowers she had taken to her mother's bedside as my grandmother lay dying that year. *I spent a long time getting them to look just right,* my mother said. *It gave me so much pleasure to do that for my mother.* In her voice rose a fresh compassion and love. My mother and her mother had not always gotten along. Standing in the kitchen with her, I felt myself wrapped in a triad of women, three generations who love and care for each other the best that they can. This is the work of women, women who do not forget.

I was unsure when it had happened, but my mother had become a flower-bringer.

Today in my studio I can hear no fluttering and chatter from the finches. I look up from my desk and rise to thrust my head out the door. The wind has indeed dropped. The surface of the Earth looks almost soft again. The finches knew before I did. I want to call them back, to tell me what I need to hear over and over again: that spring follows winter, that beauty takes many forms and that the light of a spirit can never be lost.

The Western culture in which I live says little or nothing to acknowledge the feminine cycles of the Earth, or the healing rhythms of the human heart. I wonder whatever happened to the divine creative energy of the Graces, the Fates and the Muses, not to mention all the other female spiritual figures who still inform and support the practices of many Eastern faiths: women who are models of nurturing, truth or compassion, whose arms encompass and enclose with softness and ease.

I look around my muddy and still dormant garden in search of the triple goddess, the Great Mother, Demeter, Divine Mother, *la mer* becoming *la mère*, the mother of all water, swimming and brimming with life, flowing like the Saraswati River, bringing forth a lush, loving world. Soon, I will know her maternal presence most vividly in delicate spring blossoms that fill the air with a sweet scent. She comes to me every year in this way, as a charming flower-bringer entwined in a scarf blown by a cosmic wind, as a sustaining miracle rising up from dark, rich loam, as a desire too large to hold.

SPRING 2007

CODA

I LIVED WITHIN the circular imprisonment of memory during the winter of 2001–2002. Shackled by recollections in that long, dark season, I found my way through who my mother was (and who I thought she was); through which parts of her have been lost to the illness; through which parts remain even near the end of her physical decline; and finally, to what she is essentially, purely. This, the most important perception of being, does not involve the mind.

For my mother, the absence of memory in her life has created its own sort of imprisonment. Sometimes, when I sit beside her, I sense her continued struggle to free herself from the bounds of forgetfulness. Memory plays its tricks on both of us, in its absence and with its weighted presence. In this way, my effort to accept what has taken place in her life has taught me that the mind, for all its potential, cannot be depended on the way the heart can. Perhaps that is why Alzheimer's – this inexplicable disease with such tragic implications for the mind – can teach so much about the heart.

My mother is now seventy-five years old and in the final stages of the disease, somewhere between 7d and 7f. She cannot walk alone. She cannot eat alone. She cannot dress or toilet herself. She no longer smiles. When she cries, during moments of great, inexpressible distress that still pass over her from time to time, she does so without tears. *Does she know you?* I am asked occasionally, by those who are unaware of the progression of losses. *No*, I reply, as patiently as I can muster, wishing that I could banish this question from the repertoire of caring inquiries. Then I continue on, in the best way I know how. *She has not known me for some time.* I offer more words to disperse the pity pinching the face of the one who has inquired. *At least not the way you and I know each other.*

She still takes food when it is offered, and she sighs in the silence. Some days, she chirps like a bird, expressing in unintelligible syllables of sound that she is, in her own way, contented. Some days, she seems agitated, troubled or tortured. Most days, she sits quietly, wrapped in the delicate fibres of her inability to remember. Eventually, the first and final memory of a human life, the knowledge of breath, will cease to circulate effectively across her neurotransmitters. She will no longer take in oxygen. And then, she will pass from this world.

Fourteen years after I consciously noticed the first signs of her illness, she is now almost completely infirm, requiring a hospital bed to reduce the possibility of bedsores, needing a wheelchair to be transported. Her material experience has shrunk to one velour-covered La-Z-Boy chair and a bed, two cushioned worlds between which she alternates, morning, afternoon and evening.

On a recent visit home, I helped my younger sister purchase sheets for our mother's new Medibed. We chose pale blue ones, to match her eyes. They would have also matched the blue hues in the quilt I made for her nine years ago, though the quilt is now worn, spotted and faded by bleach and many washings. It has been packed away. The sheets we purchased are 100% Egyptian cotton, densely woven and crisp. *Only the best for Mom,* my sister said at the store when we rummaged through the various packages to find the right size.

When we arrived in her room, my mother was ready to be transferred into the bed for the night. She was sitting in a wheelchair, slumped and silent, her eyes half-closed. We smoothed the new sheets over the bed, tucking in the corners neatly as she had taught us, plumping the pillow. Then, the caregiver helped us transfer her. As he lifted her, she grew agitated, jerking her arms and calling out a troubled stream of syllables that signaled her distress. We continued the transfer. She is now much too weak to struggle physically in a meaningful way.

As my sister lifted her legs into place on the bed and worked to arrange the sheets around them, I held onto her shoulders to keep her from tangling up in the cotton. Her hands and arms were gathered before her heart in an unconscious gesture of prayer. I clasped my hands around hers and leaned toward her, softly singing the nursery song I have taken to chanting when I visit her.

Mary had a little lamb, little lamb, little lamb.
Mary had a little lamb whose fleece was white as snow.
And everywhere that Mary went, Mary went, Mary went,
Everywhere that Mary went the lamb was sure to go.

As I sang and my sister covered her, the shivering eased. Unexpectedly, she raised her head off the pillow and opened her eyes wide. Her left eye was especially open, offering me a view through a never-ending portal of light. This was no doorway for the ordinary grasp of attachment. Startled, I shifted my eyes, turned my cheek to hers and pulled her into a hug. I began to sing the song again, whispering it this time into her ear.

My mother's illness has challenged my optimism and my faith more than any other experience in my life. And yet, by opening my heart to its painful realities, I have managed to greet the fullness of her engaging and frightening self, her wildness and her elegance, her anger and her joy, her life and her death. In my mother I have discovered the glittering bead of humanity and wholeness that is a seed of glass, at once transparent and protected, inert and alive.

Along the way, I have relocated the dreamy girl carefully counting a handful of change to see how long a necklace she could afford to string. Such are the shapes and shimmerings of the heart's beads, a strand of memories and reflections long enough to unite daughter with mother, heart with mind, spirit with its own outcome.

THE EFFORT EXHAUSTED SWANN'S BRAIN, until,
passing his hand over his eyes, he cried out: "Heaven help me!"
as people, after lashing themselves into an intellectual frenzy
in their endeavours to master the problem of the reality of the
external world, or that of the immortality of the soul, afford
relief to their weary brains by an unreasoning act of faith.

– Marcel Proust, *Swann's Way*

ACKNOWLEDGEMENTS

I AM MOST GRATEFUL to my family: my brother and sisters Timothy, Nancy and Nora, each of whom attended to the needs of our mother with generosity, dedication and perseverance; my aunt JoAnn, who shared family stories otherwise out of reach to me; my husband Timothy, who has supported me with patience, love and loyalty over these many years; and our two children – strong, energetic and inspiring – who continue to be my one true compass in an oft-tilted life.

Anything written over the course of several years and drafts develops and grows into a book only because it has been supported by others. Thanks to Theresa Kishkan, who first suggested that I read Joan Erikson's *The Universal Bead* and reviewed a very early draft of this volume. My appreciation for Kim Clarke, who inspires me in her fascination with domestic arts and lent me *From Thimble to Gown*. Leslie Jones consistently shared her enthusiasm and undying faith in this project, from the first words that hit the page. Other early readers encouraged the development of this book: Nancy Flight, Shaena Lambert, Deb Thomas, and in particular, Janice Logan. Naomi Diamond cast sharp eyes on the pages when I needed her assistance and I have had the recent privilege of working with a gifted editor, Clea McDougall. I am most grateful for Clea's quiet skill, and for the vision of the publisher and staff at timeless books. Without any of this support when it was offered, I would have been adrift.

And then there are the small mercies of a life. Thank you to Susan Andrews Grace, Val Amies, my garden and my bird feeder.

For setting out bright lanterns that have lit the path, I offer my deep appreciation to Mary Jo Fetterly, Warren Fischer, Marilyn James and Elizabeth Dey Stewart.

Thanks are due to the community where I live, a small city of many creative people who nurture and support each other. But a stone's throw away is Yasodhara Ashram, a precious place of contemplation, natural beauty and spiritual teaching. Inspiration, support and the right measure of solitude are essential to my writer's life.

With praise and admiration, I acknowledge the caregivers who have tended to my mother's spiritual and physical needs these many past years. You are the real heroes of Alzheimer's disease. Thank you.

BIBLIOGRAPHY

Anderson, Sherry Ruth and Patricia Hopkins. *The Feminine Face of God: The Unfolding of the Sacred in Women.* New York: Bantam Books, 1991.

Bolen, Jean Shinoda. *Goddess in Everywoman: Powerful Archetypes in Women's Lives.* San Francisco: Harper & Row, 1984.

Cleary, Thomas, trans. and ed. *Immortal Sisters: Secret Teachings of Taoist Women.* Berkeley, CA: North Atlantic Books, 1989.

Desikachar, T.K.V. *The Heart of Yoga: Developing a Personal Practice.* Rochester, VT: Inner Traditions, 1995.

Erikson, Joan. *The Universal Bead.* New York: W.W. Norton, 1993.

Flinders, Carol Lee. *At the Root of this Longing: Reconciling a Spiritual Hunger and a Feminist Thirst.* New York: Harper-Collins, 1998.

Hamilton, Edith. *Mythology: Timeless Tales of Gods and Heroes.* New York: New American Library, 1940.

Iyengar, Geeta S. *Yoga: A Gem for Women.* Kootenay Bay, BC: Timeless Books, 2005.

Jensen, Doreen and Polly Sargeant. *Robes of Power.* Vancouver: UBC Press, 1987.

Joyce, James. *Ulysses.* New York: Random House, 1961.

Lao-Tzu. *Tao Te Ching.* New York: Alfred A. Knopf, 1994.

Markale, Jean. *The Great Goddess: Reverence of the Divine Feminine from the Paleolithic to the Present.* Rochester, VT: Inner Traditions, 1999.

Neumann, Erich. *The Great Mother: An Analysis of the Archetype.* Trans. from German by Ralph Manheim. Princeton: Princeton University Press, 1963.

Noble, Vicki. *Motherpeace: A Way to the Goddess through Myth, Art, and Tarot.* San Francisco: Harper & Row, 1983.

Oliver, Mary. *The Leaf and the Cloud.* Cambridge, MA: Da Capo Press, 2000.

Pattabhi Jois, Sri K. *Yoga Mala.* New York: Farrar, Straus & Giroux, 1999.

Proust, Marcel. *Swann's Way.* New York: Modern Library, 1928.

Radha, Swami Sivananda. *The Divine Light Invocation.* Kootenay Bay, BC: Timeless Books, 2006.

———. *Kundalini Yoga for the West: A Foundation for Character Building, Courage and Awareness.* Kootenay Bay, BC: Timeless Books, 2004.

Shenk, David. *The Forgetting: Alzheimer's: Portrait of an Epidemic.* Bantam, Doubleday, Dell Publishing Group, 2003.

Van Gilder, Ethel. *From Thimble to Gown, A Manual of Sewing.* Boston: Allyn & Bacon, 1932.

Walker, Barbara G. *The Woman's Encyclopedia of Myths and Secrets.* San Francisco: Harper & Row, 1983.

www.kstrom.net and www.shannonthunderbird.com have provided invaluable information straight from the source about the spiritual values and cultural practices of aboriginal North Americans.

ABOUT THE AUTHOR

EILEEN DELEHANTY PEARKES writes regularly for the award-winning magazine, *ascent*. Her writing reflects her interest in landscape, cultural history, spirituality and the human imagination. Eileen is the author of *The Geography of Memory* (2002), co-author of *The Inner Green* (2005), and a contributor to *River of Memory* (2006). She received her BA from Stanford University and her MA from the University of British Columbia. Eileen lives in southeastern British Columbia and is the mother of two teenaged sons.

TIMELESS BOOKS

SINCE 2004, timeless has been committed to printing our
books on 100% Post Consumer Waste (PCW) recycled paper,
and using vegetable-based inks. We believe our environmental
commitment truly makes a difference. In this print-run of 3000
books produced on 100% PCW paper, we save 3 tons of wood
(approximately 18 trees), 1575 pounds of CO_2 (greenhouse
gases), 12 million BTUs of energy, 6536 gallons of water and
839 pounds of solid waste. *

timeless books
at the Centre for Social Innovation
215 Spadina Avenue Suite 423
Toronto, ON M5T 2C7
www.timeless.org

This book was typset in Adobe Garamond

*statistics generated by papercalculator.org